TOTAL B

AN UNAPOLOGETIC EMBRACE OF
BOSS-LIKE FEMININITY

CAI RANDOLPH

TOTAL B...

AN UNAPOLOGETIC EMBRACE OF BOSS-LIKE FEMININITY

Carlene Randolph

© 2018 Carlene Randolph

All Rights Reserved. No portion of this publication may be reproduced, stored in any electronic system, or transmitted in any form or by any means (electronic, mechanical, photocopy, recording or otherwise) without written permission from the publisher. Mild quotations may be used for literary reviews.

Disclaimer: Please note that the details included in this book are for informational purposes only. The publisher and author have made every effort to ensure the accuracy of the information contained within this book. However, they make no warranties as to the completeness of the contents herein, and hence hereby declaim any liability for errors, omissions, or contrary interpretation of the subject matter. The information contained cannot be considered a substitute for treatment as prescribed by a therapist or other professional. By reading this book, you are assuming all risks associated with using the advice, data, and suggestions given, with a full understanding that you, solely, are responsible for anything that may occur as a result of putting this information into action in any way — regardless of your interpretation of the advice.

Published in Dallas, Georgia, by
SBG Media Group and Publishing™.

ISBN 13: 978-1-7327340-4-3

Library of Congress Control Number: Pending

Also available in electronic book.

SBG Media Group and Publishing™

Dallas, GA

www.thescatterbrainedgenius.com/publishing

Introduction

Woman! It tastes as beautiful on the tongue, as it is delicate in its handling. Fierce, yet conditioned by the world to be subdued. Understanding of her own inherent strength leaves her confused because, after all, isn't 'pretty' all she's supposed to be? The feeling of uneasiness never quite leaves her. She knows she was made for more—beauty aside. The world is moving at such rapid-fire pace that what was the norm only half a century ago might be deemed abominable in today's world.

Sexism! What do we call this thing where the man rules and reigns as a monarch while the woman tends to his every whim and fancy? Never mind. It might as well be extinct because women are no longer having it! They call the shots in their own lives, as well as in those of significant others'. Gone is the woman's need to be utterly dependent on her man—or any man, for that matter—who 'calls the shots.' The desire of a woman to simply be a home-keeper was not a big deal in the past century. In fact, women didn't question their 'lot in life.' Rather than being strange, it was encouraged. But things have surely changed—as some men probably feared they would—with the surge in female education and empowerment.

All of a sudden, all over the world, a new generation of women arise who are willing to take over the world…to be 'all.' I see it on social media all the time; women who truly believe they can combine all aspects of their lives without running around crazily—and who are ready to fail some and win some. They know they don't have all the answers and that stumbling is a part of the process; however, they're also very certain that if they remain true to their innermost desires, the world will someday recognize their efforts and bow at their feet.

When a woman honors herself, all women collectively move closer to becoming what they are truly capable of being. As soon as I catch a glimpse of such a woman, I am motivated and better inclined to be all of me, instead of cowering in defeat and hiding in my own abilities and capabilities just to fit into the demographic.

I cannot be everything to everyone, but I can be everything to **ME**. Some of the people we deal with on a daily basis are a joy to be with, and their loving presence nurtures and encourages us. Others can easily influence our well-being. The concept of 'the total woman' is such a stabilizing force that by just being around her, one's disposition and morale can be completely transformed. Every man seems to know that women wield this power.

Women, though? Not as much. Women as less likely to understand the strength and incessant capabilities they possess, especially the woman who is within a certain age bracket who's not young enough to be considered 'hip,' and not old enough to be seen as 'frail.' The woman is often oblivious of her strengths while magnifying her weaknesses—all in a bid to meet up to ridiculous standards of perfection. Toxic perfectionism is what I call it. Still, the power to step back from toxicity lies within us. We can live our lives in a way that we don't end up tossing and turning in our beds in anguish, languishing in pain because of the things we know should be within our grasp but are not. Maybe we are scared that contrary to what we've been told to expect, we can be everything. We can be deep feelers and deep achievers, and it doesn't have to be one or the other.

Perhaps for me, it is easier to be achievers alone without the additional burden of soft feelings. For the woman who's true to herself, she will never be complete if she doesn't embrace her feeling-prone existence.

We will find that the moment we are honest with ourselves about our own feelings, the more candid we can be with others about how they make us feel. While this may involve some drastic changes to our social lives, it can bring about a personal transformation that will truly empower us, especially since the decision to live our truths will infuse our lives with greater happiness. If you haven't experienced such depths of freedom, perhaps it'd be difficult for you to understand or truly appreciate that anyone can feel so deeply. It would also be hard for you to know the extent to which you can flow in relieving happiness—joy that's somewhat incomprehensible to the normal person walking on the streets. The woman who was born a couple of years too early for this radical social movement of women is simply at a crossroads, unsure of where to fit in all of her ideas, creativity, and brilliance that she grew up to hide because she only wanted to show the world how pretty she is.

I am that woman, and so are you.

In this book, we are going to change wrong perceptions and deliver ourselves from mindsets that prevent us from living full, wholesome lives. This book represents today. Today, I chose to honor **ME** and **YOU**. These are challenging times for us because now that we've been liberated to pursue our dreams and to be 'all,' we just might not have been trained for it and, consequently, not know what to do. To assume we're like those 20-something-year-olds with fire in their blood, who were taught (by us) to believe they can be anything they choose to be, is a fallacy. We are not like them. We are transitionary. Akin to someone who's between making crucial life choices and who are stuck because going in one direction means completely forfeiting the other, we find ourselves lost and asking questions. Can we complain? Not really. After all, we watched the emancipation of women—and what else could give one sheer joy? The problem then becomes: How do we live and glide with emancipation? How to survive freedom?

Oh. You thought it would be a lot easier than surviving slavery? How wrong were you to think so?

You have been freed to pursue your passion. But your passion laughs at you in the face because you know next-to-nothing about its pursuit because all along, it was all in your head, as you tossed and turned every night, hoping for just a glimpse of freedom.

Isn't it disappointing that when freedom stands before you now, you stare back at it, blinking confusedly because its stranger than anything you have ever experienced?

Here's the good news: We can prepare ourselves for our passion. It's not too late to fulfill our purposes or to make good use of our drive.

Don't toss aside your life like it's a fairly-used rag. The book you hold in your two hands offers you a chance at reigniting your passion. Catch a glimpse of wholeness and never, ever move away from this sensational gift you have been given to plant in and reap from life once again!

And what if you're not 'young'? What if you aren't 'cool' or 'hip'?

There's still a place for you on the table. This place is one of wisdom; one where you can take a pool of the resources of experience garnered over the years, as you become the go-to person for all things wise and important.

You were born for such a time as this; to make **BOSS MOVES**, challenge the **STATUS QUO**, and become the replica of the **STRONG WOMAN**—the untouchable and the unparalleled paragon of emotional intelligence. The thing is this: You didn't go through so much for you to bury your head in the sands of life or to become inconsequential when important, life-changing decisions are being made regarding world affairs.

And so, this book is for you, no matter where you are on this planet Earth—the **woman** who thinks she is no longer relevant; the **mother** who feels as though motherhood robbed her of the chance to live for herself; the **woman** in the boardroom who is now unsatisfied because although she has been accorded respect that rivals that of the men in the room, unlike them, she has no home to run to because it disappeared while she was trying to make a point for the strength and ambition of women.

This book is one that shows you that stepping down on one for the other has never been and should never be the way out because you'd surely come to regret it—privately or publicly.

Table of Contents

Introduction v
Chapter 1 1
   EMBRACE THE PAIN
Chapter 2 7
   EMBRACE THE SILENCE
Chapter 3 13
   CATHARSIS: EMBRACE THE OPENNESS
Chapter 4 34
   EMBRACE HELPFULNESS
Chapter 5 55
   MAKING BOSS MOVES IN CHALLENGING TIMES
Chapter 6 67
   EMBRACING THE POWER TO STEP BACK FROM TOXICITY
Chapter 7 72
   EMBRACING POSITIVE PEOPLE INTO YOUR SPACE
Chapter 8 76
   EMBRACING YOU: BEING ALL YOU CAN BE
Chapter 9 89
   EMBRACING CONTINUAL EXCELLENCE
Chapter 10 94
   EMBRACING FORGIVENESS
Conclusion 100

Carlene Randolph

Chapter 1

EMBRACE THE PAIN

You Will Go Through it, Not Around It

I see women in pain all the time. It's the kind of gnashing pain that is rhetorically silent. The thing is: I don't see it as much as I **FEEL** it. Of course, a lot of other people might not be able to feel it as acutely; perhaps because they haven't been in the shoes of those women. But, oh: I sure have!

Can we talk? Like woman-to-woman talk—baring our souls and all, daring to speak of the pain we face and lending our voices to our own causes, instead of choosing to bury the other woman in the hope that it'd make us feel better about ourselves...plights and all?

Pain. In its raw, untarnished form, pain has the innate potential to be beautiful. It is alluring and far more rewarding when unraveled (rather than buried), with the assumption that all it has come to do is destroy our lives. Change our lives, it will; but the pain is more of a birther than it is a destroyer.

As women—middle-aged women, in particular—we've seen it all. We know how pain envelops us and have been in situations when our pain made us incapable of succeeding at our crafts—when it weakened us so much, we resolved to get revenge through whatever means we deemed fit. And we go to the other side—sometimes through sheer determination, and other times with the aid of people who pushed and pushed and pushed through for us.

If we are truthful, though, we all know there's some unresolved pain lurking in our minds. Some, we've chosen to shut out of our lives as we make 'solid' attempts at moving on.

Perhaps if we saw the pain as part of our stories instead of some outside influence trying to break us, we could be all-inclusive and bring this pain into our overall thoughts, building up ourselves even through it.

"Don't see, don't search, don't ask, don't know, don't demand—relax. If you relax, it comes. If you relax, it is there. If you relax, you start vibrating with it." ~Osho~

It's been a long time for me, but for as long as I've known, pain has been a part of me that I cannot ignore. And so, I would pore and pore over each detail of my pain, trying to find out its origin and pinpoint the source of this unending battle with emotional pain.

For so long, I persisted in thinking sessions, searching for answers that always seems to elude me. If I came up with those answers, I would surely find peace—or so it occurred to my already-bewildered mind. Had I committed some heinous, unforgivable offense, that my own life was singled out for trauma and pain without end?

Life had victimized me, doubling me up in pain at every single moment. Pain which, even if I tried to get relief from by using the strongest concoction of pain-relief medication, still wouldn't abort the agony.

And so, in an attempt at combating this overwhelming pain, I battled them with positive emotions. This I did in a mechanical fashion. Rather than accept the fact that some staunch negativity lurched within me, I chose to use positivity as the barrier that chased away suffering at all costs. It was my means of defending myself against the pain.

You know, it seems (in retrospect) laughable, but that means I did not try to convert a negative feeling into a full-blown positive one. To what extent didn't I go to make this pain reverberating within my person disappear and be replaced with a blanket of reasonable possibility? The funny thing is that just like someone whose pain was refusing the attention of pain-relievers, mine seemed to echo loudly in my ears, cackling rather disturbingly.

Then, it happened.

The transformation I describe to you—the one I wish for you to take heart so deeply, so transformative in its nature that every other thing pales in its wake. I received permission to embrace my pain. The knowledge came that assured me my pain was not a bad thing; that it was freedom at its peak. In embracing my pain, I could find wholeness that wrapped me in solid joy. Finally, I had the freedom to forgive myself and grieve the distress and shock which I'd held within my mind, bound in the shackles of my being.

No, it wasn't easy. I don't think it ever could have been easy to look my pain in the face and walk through it.

But this was the only real solution. I had to go **THROUGH** it. Not around it. Not in front of it. Not behind it. It sunk me for a minute, as the pain consumed me. I felt it in the deepest crevices of my soul, and I attempted to turn back—but seeing as I had gotten this far, I chose to push through, and oh, it engulfed me. Even as I think about it, I remember those moments too clearly, perhaps because pain is one of the deepest emotions ever felt by man.

When I truly allowed myself to ruminate on my pain, I saw that I'd been holding onto thoughts that were harmful—beliefs that other people were responsible for my pain. I held to my belief that I wasn't the one at fault for the pain I felt; other people were. I was the victim in those situations. How could I ever achieve inner peace with that thought pattern?

If I recently (or not-so-recently) experienced a break-up, it automatically became the fault of my ex-man that my life was in shambles. Who else to blame, you know? My last break-up was climacteric—the pain banging in my ears, much louder than any I'd experienced prior. Funny: I thought if I hated him enough, maybe the pain I felt within would be less.

Finally, it clicked! By once again avoiding my pain, I was swimming against the tide—and we all know how dangerous that is. Why did I find it so easy to ruminate on my happiness, but rather impossible to accept my loneliness, pain, and sadness wholly?

I forgot one simple fact: All emotions have come to teach us; none without fail. If I could embrace all of life, I'd definitely grow more and become wholesomely experienced. It was at this realization that I finally stopped seeking someone to blame for any adverse situation that affected me.

And so, as I embrace my pain, I begin to heal and grow in ways I never thought possible prior. As I embrace my turmoil, while still shining a light on my soul, I observe the true depth of the darkness in my heart. I know that what I am being given, I can cope with, and so, I learn to go with the flow.

We can't keep going against the flow and expect to be fulfilled. In embracing our pain, we learn that all of a sudden, the pain doesn't last for long. It is transient. And it doesn't hurt forever.

Chapter 2

EMBRACE THE SILENCE

It Doesn't Hurt; It Heals

Carlene Randolph

Calculated beauty isn't really beauty at all. It is, perhaps, a sullied version of beauty, one in which our quest to find out what could have been—and, indeed, was—we coin. The beautiful poem by Rainer Maria Rilke comes to mind:

> *"Let your beauty manifest itself*
> *without talking or calculation.*
> *You are silent.*
> *It says for you: I am.*
> *And comes in meaning thousand-fold,*
> *comes at long last over everyone."*

It's becoming extra difficult to 'take a shot of silence.' Like with so much noise in the external environment, engulfing us and demanding of us, the vital moments of our day, we are all but lost in the motions of the day. As this happens time and again, we become scared of the revelations which silence brings us. How can we cope with being alone when being alone means we have to face all our fears in the now-imposed silence of our minds?

And so, we choose noise. Perhaps this was the arbitrary origin of the noise in our environment—the music blaring at inner-ear jarring tones and beyond reasonably audible levels (this musician was trying to escape from silence maybe?); the buzz of the alarm clocks forcing us to rationally adhere to our time schedules; people conversing in sharp, loud, insensitive tones. We get used to the noise.

Total B...

We weren't made in noise. Rather, when we were formed, we were protected from noise. Your first cry was a protest against being thrown into an environment completely different from the life you were used to in your mother's womb.

As you become older, external noise transfers into internal noise. Your mind begins to weave thoughts together, as you deliberate on how capable, how loving, how great (and, on the contrary, how not-so-great) you are. How can we experience silence when we are always so conscious of the endless mind and physical chatter going on in and around us?

For women, the situation even borders on being worse.

See, whether you want to think about your beauty or not, everything forces you to consider your looks. From the incessant position on the beauty that most ads churn out, to the massive favors the beautifully-born ones get, you soon learn the easiest way to get what you want is by having features that are pleasing to the eyes. No, you don't have to do anything. You just have to 'BE.' Be beautiful enough. Thinking about that and trying to attain those standards endlessly can be a chore.

It certainly dissuades you from the posture of silence. We all can be sure that silence is, indeed, a virtue that's as all-encompassing as time.

Just before the age-long creation of man, the world was in silence. The universe remained an open, vast space; the only things echoing in the distance being stillness, quietness, and utmost tranquility. Silence doesn't search for validity: It simply 'IS.' For that reason in itself, silence will always remain beautiful. I think we forget how important silence is to our beings, which is why many of us don't get silence imprinted on our beings early enough and why it doesn't come naturally for us.

Otherwise, why do we feel uneasy when there's a pause in action? Why are we afraid of otherwise normal gaps that come during conversations, seeking to always fill them up with 'sentence fillers' and awkward laughter? More than that, we also tactically avoid those moments when noise is absent. That is when it becomes obvious how afraid we really are of silence. If our generation already fears silence, think how much harder it will be for those behind us to be able to tolerate its beautiful nuances. After all, they never get it as a 'thing.' It's always been foreign to them.

And so, I have no choice but to wonder: How possible is it to make room for silence in our technology-crazed world? What are we missing out on, as we choose to run away from the beauty of silence?

Funny enough, silence isn't all that hard to find. It's everywhere around us—if we care enough to look for it. When we make deliberate, calculated steps to find silence, we discover that it removes the tension that's so palpable all around us and, as well, we can readily recharge our inner batteries! I can't be the only one who's felt so much better after lying on my bed and soaking in moments of silence all around me!

Total B...

While amidst the need for you to change the kids' diapers and run off to the grocery store to get things for the house—all in addition to a busy career and actually being 'there' for your family—silence might seem like an archaic, unimportant word that means nothing to you. On the contrary, it is the only true stabilizing force in your life. Thinking of how to bring silence into your day? Here are some tips:

- Focus on your breath. Breathe in and out over and over again.
- Pick a corner in your house that can serve as your 'quiet zone'—your sanctuary where you can create a journal without being disturbed.
- Where do you take your morning coffee? In front of a television? Nope. Don't do that. Sip it on the patio next time.
- As you drive, focus all of your attention on the road, rather than on that music blaring out of your radio. If you have to switch off the radio, do it.
- Don't speak so forcefully. Organize your thoughts, then bare them out in the open.
- Meditate peacefully.
- Go hiking or take a jog.
- When did you last enjoy a quiet evening without being disturbed by the phone or computer? Shut them down for a while.
- Let your mind 'be' without forcing thoughts onto it; thoughts of the present, the past, or even the future. Just 'be.'
- You know those moments right before you drift off to sleep? Truly enjoy them.

What do I love the most about silence? The chance it offers to right the wrongs of our ever-active minds. The ability to hear ourselves breathe, think, and speak—without the use of our voices. Silence is healing and will never go out of fashion.

And, as Wayne Dyer right said, *"It's really the space between the notes that makes the music you enjoy so much."*

Maybe our lives would be so much more enjoyable if we learned to savor the space between the notes of our existence. Perhaps we wouldn't be so needy, clingy, and desirous of external validation if we decided to receive all of our validation from within, instead of giving that power to other people who, depending on their moods or personality, would choose to trample upon us or make us feel incompetent—thus further perpetuating the cycle of validation-seeking behaviors.

Chapter 3

CATHARSIS: EMBRACE THE OPENNESS

Laughter and Tears

I know we all like to strut around like we feel no pain, like being strong is defined by how much you can fling aside the pain you feel and appear whole to the rest of the world. In the process of equating vulnerability with weakness, we forget that if you're ever vulnerable, you can never exhibit true, unflinching strength.

We forget that emotional clarity is lost on us when we're unable to explore our vulnerabilities as strengths rather than weaknesses.

Feeling is **NOT** a weakness. Rather, it has been exploited to suggest weakness. The only way you can find joy is by surrendering to your feelings, instead of mounting resistance against them. Embracing or encouraging painful emotions can seem like an ironic thing to say, but the alternative option is way worse. By ignoring these emotions, we set ourselves up to strengthen them and make them last.

"Your joy is your sorrow unmasked. And the selfsame well from which your laughter rises were oftentimes filled with your tears. The deeper your sorrow carves into your being, the more joy you can contain."

Someone who feels ill-fated about being unhappy will remain unhappy.

Because women are more attuned to their feelings, they almost have the monopoly of being engulfed in their negative emotions. Take, for example, Nora (real name was withdrawn) who, one day, found herself completely soaked in tears. She was at a loss as to why she was crying so much. There was no explanation for her sudden bout of tears. For this reason, she decided to speak with a doctor. After all, she was losing her mind!

Together, on further probing and questioning, the doctor helped Nora see how much her mind was more aware of her life than she was. The reason for her sad feelings was because she ought to have delivered a child, whose pregnancy happened to have been terminated earlier. Her whole being was grieving for her loss, and she didn't even know it! Having this knowledge enabled her to overcome these negative emotions. She accepted the grief—and went through it, not around it.

Finally, after successfully going through the grief, Nora found acceptance and emotional release. She was finally free from the incapacitating emotions that befell her only a few moments before.

What I'm trying to say is that emotions always have a flipside. There's no such thing as a vacuum with regards to emotions. There's a bimodal spectrum: On the other end of anxiety is calmness while, on the other end of confusion, is clarity. Anger has on its other end, acceptance; while joy replaces sadness or grief, just as contentment replaces discontent.

How, then, can you encourage the development of the positive spectrum of emotions while discouraging the negative ones? The answer might seem cliché:

There's no other option than to go through it to get to the other side.

You'd discover that when you overcome the resistance to going through those emotions and merely choose to flow through them, you'd achieve a state of release sooner than later and then: **BOOM!** You're flowing in the positive!

I have never encouraged people to just 'forget about pain'; neither do I trivialize the things that make tears well up in the eyes of others. Why? Because you can never tell how much pain it is causing them. These painful emotions often correlate with feelings or threat of loss.

If you choose to numb those feelings by ignoring them and focus, instead, on wild partying, drinking, or knocking yourself out with one addiction or another, you will find that you have achieved nothing. Those feelings will **NOT** disappear when you return; they're still there!

I always advise women to bring their inner demons out in the open and to face them head-on.

The Instinct for Survival Through Emotional Hardship.

You think you've gotten to the end of your rope, right? Wrong. Man wasn't made to give up so easily. It might surprise you to find that resilience has been so deeply rooted in your being, it'd take so much for you to finally give up on living!

This brings to mind the great author, Viktor Frankl—a Viennese doctor and psychologist—who was the director of a hospital's Neurology department at the time Hitler's National Socialists invaded Austria in 1938.

As was the case of many, Viktor was arrested (in 1942). His offense? He was Jewish. He was kept in a concentration camp, separated from his wife and family.

After long periods of unbeknownst suffering, Viktor survived the gruesome experience to tell the story in his book, *Man's Search for Meaning*, and went on to live for about 50 years, before dying at the ripe, old age of 92. His book sold millions and millions of copies because it resonated profoundly with the minds of readers.

Throughout his detention and up until he was freed, Viktor kept making ground-shattering psychological inferences, allowing his mind to churn out ideas on survival—using himself as a case study—and finally adding flesh to the subject matter of Logotherapy, a form of understanding he had been working on before he was detained. This Logotherapy had, as its major focus, the idea that one can find meaning in life, despite terribly tempting scenarios that threaten life; and, as such, maintain the desire to live.

It was unbelievable! The extent to which man would hold on tenaciously to the desire and will to live, regardless of the trauma that befell him.

When Frankl was arrested, life had been predictably going well for him. He had a home, career, dreams, and ambitions. He also had just gotten married to the love of his life. Things couldn't have been rosier—and then, he was forced to give all of that up!

Predictably, Frankl went into a bout of denial. In his description of his experiences, he rightly-describes how he felt in those initial periods; the feeling of false hope or the illusion of reprieve lasted for a short period. The man was huddled with other strangers, and they went on a journey to a large internment camp where several prisoners who looked like they had no hope marched around the building. The new intake of prisoners was made to drop their luggage and walk towards a certain direction, before being further subdivided by how strong they looked. Prisoners (like Frankl) who looked 'strong' were kept alive, while others were killed almost immediately. To preserve his life, Frankl had to say goodbye to his beloved manuscript on Logotherapy. This was when he finally had to accept that his life had completely changed and that the reality he now faced was totally different from what he knew. In his words, he 'struck out his former life.'

Next, the men had to undress completely, and all of their hair (including their eyebrows!) was shaved. The only thing left with Frankl was his pair of shoes and spectacles. For the next three years, his life was filled with varying degrees of hardship, terror, and pushing on with a strong will to survive.

Imagine a scenario where all the things you loved to do were forcibly taken from you! It becomes almost impossible to live through those moments, as so much has been taken away from you regarding your personality, control, feelings, and dignity. You think that's such a far cry from what could happen today, right? People still go through such terrible circumstances.

For example, there are people—the world over—who have their peaceful habitats shaken by natural disasters such as famines, droughts, hurricanes, and volcanic eruptions. And so, they have to begin their lives anew.

Imagine being diagnosed with some untreatable disease like cancer or being told your life was over and you had only a few weeks to live as your internal clock ticks. The hospital becomes your home, you no longer have a face, and different treatments have become your lot. You have been stripped all the way down to the very essentials (who thinks of makeup when you're being told the chemotherapy you're being loaded with would lead to the loss of all your hair, even your eyebrows?). Some things simply fade into the distance. Even when people you love are all around you, you probably feel alone, helpless. And frightened.

The doctors try to provide treatment and even make jokes, but when you look deeply enough into their eyes, you see that they, too, are scared silly. They can administer chemotherapy or radiotherapy, but they cannot promise you life or hope. They can talk about 'this' or 'that' patient who miraculously has no trace of cancer in their bone marrow, but you see a worried crease on their brows as if to say, "But what if the patient has a relapse?"

One significant mark of hope is the ability to maintain humor in the face of such depressing circumstances. When all is lost, humor should be retained.

For Frankl and his other gang of prisoners, that was one thing they were not lost on. They found that they were laughing with each other, and now that there was nothing else to lose, they could laugh at one another—bonding in their unpalatable grief and echoing the aliveness of their human spirits. It was the onset of their desires to help one another get through these trying times and otherwise hopeless existence.

This further reinforced the truth in the folk saying that a day devoid of laughter and tears was a day wasted! Laughter and tears are cathartic forms that give us the needful connections between the false and true versions of our realities. It was also a very important aspect of our emotional healing.

Why do we laugh or cry?

We do so when some truth stabs our mind, and we have no choice but to look into and burst the bubble of denial we had been living in. As we finally let go of the falseness we had been holding onto, we might find that we burst into an uncontrollable bout of laughter.

The process of giving up our stronghold of such false beliefs might be so stressful that we tremble and cry, as we have no choice but to give it up. The spectrum of emotions we, therefore, go through could include: shame, anger, fear, and confusion. But we eventually cry, as we finally let it go.

The path to healing has been briefly described. As we release the energies bound in our likes, dislikes, hopes, fears, anger, and happiness, we can gain restoration. The first law of Thermodynamics helps us note that energy can never be created nor destroyed; it can only be transformed from one form into another. In this way, healing leads to growth. As we survive one loss, we become wiser and can understand our strengths, weaknesses, and paths we shouldn't follow anymore.

Also, survival in one area makes you able to face another loss with great confidence! Similar losses no longer move you as they used to before. You become free to experience emotions in their full length, at heightened intensities. In this way, you become very 'alive.'

For the prisoners who were with Frankl, their laughter (I'd like to think) was not just because they wanted to poke fun at one another; it was also because they felt a sense of relief they didn't think possible, especially when considering their new, unfortunate circumstances.

This is a viable point to how we feel when everything is taken away from us—thus, leaving us with a conscious awareness of ourselves. Who we are. How we glide. How we feel. Our emotions. Our creative impulses. All serve to make us able to truly 'feel.'

The shower in itself was cleansing. Feeling such cool water on uncovered flesh after long hours on the road is restorative. It's comforting. It, therefore, allows you to focus on the simple realities of your life—on simply **'BEING.'**

Mindfulness comes to the forefront here. It reminds you of whom you are.

Memories formed in your soul are long-lasting, eternal, and they come to the forefront when things happen that spur them to the surface. This is probably one other reason the men burst into uncontrolled laughter on that first day, eyebrows and all hair shaved off. They had no choice but to make contact with their souls.

The same happens when you are placed in a hospital ward or fall suddenly ill, being forced to stay in bed for a period of compulsory bedrest. It happens when you no longer have a choice regarding running away from harsh, existential circumstances. There's no means of escape or wriggling out, so do what you have to do. If you must survive, you have to go through it. In this situation, you have to choose if you'd rather survive or if you won't (i.e., this is what it means when you decide to be alive and live regardless of what happens). No one can make you happy or unhappy without your consent. It's called a 'choice' for a reason.

Many of those who survived the initial Nazi culls finally ran into electricity-charged fencing and died. Instead of choosing to go further, they simply chose death. Frankl, on the other hand, chose not to commit suicide from that very first day in the camp—a decision which truly required boldness. Deciding to live was quite hard because what he had to choose next was how to deal with the hunger in the camp. As much as they couldn't get more food, they also had to learn to keep the little bit of strength they had. They also helped one another to take care of their physiques by removing all forms of infestations from their skin, helping them to sleep better and preventing them from having infections.

Friendship was also crucial to their survival because if you didn't feel good on a particular day, another person could help you feel better. But what if your friend was killed the next day? And hence, it became their instincts to protect each other from the things that hurt them during their daily activities and duties. Nonetheless, they also needed moments of quietness, to refuel and keep hope alive. All of these are important in growth and, as they were needed for Frankl, you need them as well.

Embracing openness requires that you love the next person as much as you love yourself and that you think their lives are as important as you view yours. This is quite similar to friendship, but still, is different! It is called 'identifying with the suffering of others.' As you have experienced laughter and tears with others, you come into a firm understanding of the similar joys and sorrows that you face and, as such, you're both able to relate immediately.

These intimate relations create a feeling of importance in you both and, as you've got your friend's back, she has yours, too. Knowing this strengthens you and helps you to know that even when you fall or fail, someone else will be there to raise you up. This requires a strong degree of vulnerability with the people in your lives who face similar circumstances as you.

Can you think of anyone who's in the same boat as you are? Even without directly considering helping one another stay afloat, the truth is that it comes naturally to us to do so— even though mentally, those identifications might be taken for granted. Yet, these attachments are what form deep definitions of our beings, and which eventually control our actions and inactions.

As the philosopher in Gibran said, "The selfsame well from which your laughter rises were oftentimes filled with your tears." It is possible, as well, that what makes you happy today could be the source of your uncontrollable tears tomorrow.

Those people in your life who form a strong base of companionship are, therefore, worthy of being guarded against pain because when you have them, you surely know they can also shield you against the same sort of pain. By protecting them in a way, you also protect yourself. In times of glaring pain, it is this ability to play, make jokes, and focus on the joys around you that will pull you out of despair.

Emotional Injury and the Circumstances Needed for Healing.

From Frankl, you can draw from him the knowledge of what you need to be completely healed of every emotional hurt. Besides the camaraderie of his newly-acquired friends and teammates, what made it possible for him to survive was the knowledge of the love shared amongst himself and his wife. It was almost akin to the love which many of these people were familiar with, knowing it to have come from God—thus, helping them to maintain their spiritual beliefs. He came to understand that for every one of us, love is the highest ideal to which we can aspire. With the love he knew was present between himself and his wife, he was just too sure that love could keep a man alive, even when he had nothing else working in his favor.

In his words: "I grasped the meaning of the greatest secret that human poetry and human thought and belief have to impart. The salvation of man is through love and in love. I understood how a man who has nothing left in the world still may know bliss."

Emotional hurt requires love as an environment in which it's to have complete healing; just as much as an open wound needs to be well-cleansed and free of all forms of infections. If need be, antibiotics will be prescribed. Emotional hurts require the environment of love to truly heal.

The love I refer to here is that form of selfless love which you know is present for you, regardless of what happens in the external environment; not necessarily the type that aims to possess and make you inaccessible to others. It is not the passionate love that comes with desire, but rather the divine love that makes you feel secure—one which is never present, even when you go out of line or fumble through the right steps to take. Even as a 'strong' woman, you **NEED** to have this kind of love in your life. You can depend on yourself (that much, I know) but without this, you would always be hiding portions of your heart behind the shadows, too scared to allows to peep beyond the surface, always trying to cover up your need with a falsetto version of strength the world may see and believe but deep down, you know is all a façade.

How long will you maintain the lie?

Going through pain might have made you less readily-accepting of love, but what if you chose to open your arm to love that comes your way? What if you chose to listen for the kind of accepting love that isn't coming to change you, but rather build you and reassure you? What if, like Frankl, you allow yourself to reach an epiphany where you can finally appreciate your true, ancient soul? And what if you finally allow deep wisdom to shine through you, as you encounter a form of love that transcends the physical?

There's nothing wrong with yearning for love. As humans, we have been wired to want love—and rightly so. It is a vital part of our beings that need expression and validation, even. You can't even grasp the fullness of this entry by merely thinking about or contemplating on it; you've got to feel it deeply. It has to resonate deeply within your being.

It is also in moments of painful stillness that you finally appreciate what was adjudged 'normal' for you at a point—what, for you, seemed 'not so special.'

Total B...

Much like mountain peaks glow in the sunset, a transfixed feeling that goes all the way to the soul and is sometimes manifest in physical reality forces you (for a moment) to stop in your tracks and asks you—no: **COMMANDS** you—to evaluate it. It keeps you in that transfixed state from which you have no escape and no mercy. It is a moment of hope; one which implores that you stand still as it fills you with love, awe, surrender, acceptance, happiness, gratefulness, and, more than anything else, fills you up. You feel complete.

Yet, this is what you've been running away from because (I must warn you) coming to this point exposes you to yourself and can bring you to the brink of tears. But is passes! No matter how severe a period of suffering might have been, when it passes and offers you a chance to rebuild, you can be happy again—if you will take the chance, that is.

For Frankl, it took only a week and two days post-survival for him to churn out all the details that would make for a best-selling work of art in the form of a book, as he recounted all the pain, suffering, and depths of understanding he gained from each of them. As love helped him live within the internment camps, it also helped him survive his post-internment tragic pains—for his wife and the rest of his family had been murdered in the Holocaust. He would later fall in love with another beautiful woman; a hospital worker in the facility where he became Director of the Neurological Policlinic.

Could he have held onto his profound hurt and refused to heal? Absolutely. When chances provide us with healing and to move on, we can claim a lack of desire for moving on, as we can act like the mere thought of doing so is criminal. But to what end is that? We only hurt ourselves even more.

Each of us is on a journey, headed in the direction of spiritual freedom and maturity. Sometimes, we lose out on things we thought we couldn't do without. What keeps us sane is the (sometimes harsh) possibility of replacement. You needn't feel as though you are doing something wrong by replacing another who was once dear to your heart. Their memories (if they're dead) wouldn't' want you to fill them with grumpiness all in the name of missing them! "You might as well go out and have a life!" I can almost hear your dead husband implore of you. In fact, the cure for such illnesses and depression would need double-doses of love, the feeling of it, and the knowledge of it. And, of course, the mature rather than the immature form of it. Having an immature form of love is more hurtful than it is healing.

This is the story of a woman like you and me. She endured pain in several forms and now, experiences true love.

As a child, Brenda's parents were poor. As most poor people do, they trained her to keep quiet about their issues, to be grateful for even the most minimalistic thing done for her, and to accept any affliction poured on her— as though they were normal and she caused it.

So, to Brenda, life was about helping her mother and looking after her younger siblings. She was forbidden to spend ample time playing with friends or forming any type of important relationships that other children often made with classmates and playmates. Not long after, as soon as she was a teenager, she had to leave school and began to make money for the family because her parents thought her old enough to do so. It was while in this line of living that she met a young man, Brandon, who seemingly took a liking to her. Based on the kind of love she thought she knew, he provided her with something she equated to love. After all, once in a while, he told her he loved her.

She began to live with him and, as a drunk, he would sometimes beat her, was unfaithful to her, and, to cap it off, was possessive and couldn't stand her being near another man, even if it was for work-related purposes. Where could Brenda go, even if she considered leaving this man? Certainly not her parents' home, as they would never accept her back. So, she put up with his antics and prayed every day that she wouldn't end up being beaten by him once more.

Sadly, she had several miscarriages, even though she badly wanted a child whom she could completely love and nurture. One pregnancy eventually entered well into the second trimester. She was so happy that finally, the baby would stay in her womb. Her jealous and callous husband beat her so badly, she went into premature labor and lost her baby.

Having been trained against the expression of her feelings, Brenda simply moved on to the next marriage, hoping for a better outcome this time. She shouldn't have hoped much.

She would spend so many years on her own, somehow surviving. As she approached her 40s, she began working in a home for disabled, less-fortunate kids. They drew out a part of her she'd long buried; the part of her that loved to laugh and was filled with warmth. Her laughter was one which drew the attention of the widower next door, who would eventually pursue her, win her heart, and become the one with whom she could relax and finally have a home—with his two kids.

Truth be told, there was no reason anymore for Brenda to be unhappy. Still, she found that she was constantly in tears. Loss of energy, low mood, and reduced energy in previously pleasurable activities were things she found to be her default mode. And so, she had to be referred for psychiatric evaluation. It was after much deliberation that she finally spoke out about how, despite everything going well for her in recent times, she couldn't shake off the feelings of sadness and fear that regularly accosted her now. She didn't lack money, love, or any other thing for that matter. So, why, of all times, was she crying now?

She would later discover that those tears were because she was mourning her old self. She was crying because now, she was allowed to cry. She couldn't have done so in her past because she wasn't availed the opportunity to do so.

Now that she felt safe, her reservoir of thoughts and emotions thought it necessary for her to pour out all those emotions she had bottled up in the past; emotions she was completely dissuaded from expressing because along with them, came the need to mop them up. No one was available to do so for her or even to be present as she walked around in her hot mess. She cried for her miscarriages; for the babies in her womb she'd lost, for the lack of love in her family, for the fact that she had to stop schooling, for the pain she felt in both of her marriages, and for each and every pain she had bottled up that had been stored somewhere in the recesses of her mind.

Her tears were liberating for the parts of her heart that were closed off by her mind that needed (at minimum) some sort of protection before all of it was gone. Finally, it was if she had been jolted awake by the love shown her first by the disabled kids, and now, by her new family. Now that she was secure in this love and knew none of it would be snatched from her hands, she was awake.

This is a poignant reminder for all of us that eventually, we must wake up to face not only the suffering but also the happier aspects of life. It's funny how pain is often programmed to come before bliss, how winter precedes spring, and how lousy weather often precedes the beautiful scenery. But, as we face the foul seasons of life, it programs us to open our arms to the good things of life. Imagine what happens when you turn your back against the terrible seasons of your life. You would still be hiding when good seasons come along and end up feeling sad because there wouldn't be any respite. As painful and relentless as sad moments may seem, as you go through them, you see that it is a pain that finally heals you. The pain in itself becomes the drug coating in which your happiness was wrapped and, as you swallow it, you find healing.

This is the real form of catharsis. No matter how prolonged it is, when you get to the end of the road, you'd know that you've finally made it to the end of the spectrum and that you're whole. Unbelievably whole.

This is what makes me confident enough to tell you to shed those tears. Embrace the pain, instead of claiming to be badass and then shelling it up against another day, as you navigate through daily activities and gravitate towards what you consider to be 'achievements.' Without the aid of this cathartic process, you might never enjoy untroubled happiness because your joy would always be dented by the pain you know you feel but are somewhat unable to express in words.

If you go through it, I promise that you will be well. Cry. Groan. Weep, over and over again, as you drain your inner stores of pain. You needn't feel ashamed because you feel bad. Release yourself to actually feel bad! Every tear you shed lessens your tank of misery and drags you closer to the emptiness of that well of sadness.

If you can, by all means, talk to someone about it, and you will see that the more you do, the less you feel like they are the cause of your pain. You actually release them from your mind because you know they were only acting as they could, given the circumstances in which they found themselves. You will be happy—but remember that in this cathartic process, you must forgive those who have hurt you. You might not even know how much you hate them right now, but as you go on this journey, it exposes your mind so that you'd see how much hatred you had kept in your mind about them and how much you hold them accountable for your pain.

Finally, you arrive at the crossroads where you have to either release them and move on or hold onto them and continue to feel the pain. You haven't come this far to hold onto what caused you pain…I hope. It would make the entire journey fruitless.

So, cry if you must. Cry. Release your pent-up emotions. For as Gibran made us see, "The deeper your sorrow carves into your being, the more joy you can contain." He also says, "Your pain is the breaking of the shell that encloses your understanding."

Carlene Randolph

Chapter 4

EMBRACE HELPFULNESS

And the Art of Letting Go When We Can't Help

Total B...

Emotions. Emotions seem to defy logic at times, but so used are we to logic that it appears damning to choose to treat emotional crises as its own 'stand-alone' entity. And so, we rush about it as we would for medical emergencies. We find it super difficult to attune ourselves to the feelings which others are so painfully experiencing.

You only need to have been in the Intensive Care Unit once or twice to understand what I talk about when referring to the management of medical emergencies. The rapid-fire alarm responses to someone who has had a cardiac arrest, needing resuscitation. And sometimes, to the view of a learned onlooker, much of the fuss is over nothing—for we simply know that the woman whom you try so frantically to resuscitate is far gone (regarding death), but a cardiac massage would be in order, right? Even if ribs are cracking beneath the force of the resuscitating hands, the knowledge that there's a will for you to live beneath all that force should be somewhat cheering...or not?

In the process of willing someone to live, I think practitioners of medicine are apt sometimes to forget that, try as they can, they can only **TRY**. The decision of whether or not the person would live is, sadly, not up to them. You might then ask, "What is the purpose of trying?" Well, if someone were to live, for example, their efforts would be excellent in helping that person promptly come back to life. It is for this reason that they are essential.

Sometimes, it is the concept of providing heroic treatment that's at work. Using a knife for an emergency tracheotomy—a step which, if not used within the right boundaries, can easily slip from being heroic to being potentially fatal and, ultimately, lead to the death of the said person.

You know, some of the regular procedures carried out today—like renal transplants and dialysis—were once thought to be so fatal that most people who had it were candidates for death almost on the spot. The hero in this scenery is probably that person who chooses to go through any length to see that the person for whom they are providing such treatment to ends up being well! It is greatly appealing to people who are in such fields because it deems you fit to be called a 'savior.'

But we must ask ourselves if this is the right approach for non-medical purposes (i.e., psychological or emotional pain). When we want to help others so much that we become the 'hero' in the picture, is our help that badly needed, or should we step aside for a while?

You cannot use the 'emergency model' to 'snatch a friend out of the grips of death' in a rather enthusiastic desire to help them through whatever pain they might be passing through. This is not to say your fellow woman doesn't need your help but aren't there better ways to render this help than by being forceful about it? Still, it is what we know and how we have been brought up to respond to the emergencies of others; yet it shows a culture of helplessness. The desire of many of us, when we get someone deemed an 'expert' in 'this' or 'that' field, is to give up all parts of our health to that person to take care of us. Because we are apt to do this, we think other people also need to surrender themselves to us when we find ourselves in the role of 'helper.'

This isn't good for either party. As much as you can help, you would more often than not (if you would successfully help someone out) have to step back and allow the person you're trying to help to go through some reflective introspection, just so that both of you can now be on the same page.

This is not restricted to helping your fellow woman. You might find yourself engaged in heroism as you try to 'protect' your kids against harm, going to extreme measures like locking them in, beating them up, and sometimes denying them some basic needs just to prove a point to them and have them join your camp. Even husbands do so to their wives. A majority of the men who beat up their wives do so because they think they aren't listening—and, of course, believe that as the husband, they know better.

When nothing else seems to be working, we revert to forceful help as the only way out.

But have we considered the alternative? Walking away or giving up on helping altogether?

It sounds cowardly and not nearly as heroic as the doctor who slashes through a man's chest to stop him from going into laryngospasm, but what if there was no indication for that? What if, in his enthusiasm to help, he takes the heroism a bit too far and, in the process, causes more harm than good to the patient?

Our heroism might draw us to yell out in frustration at people we are trying to help, but try we must to control these impulses. Drastic, unsolicited help is often not as charming as it seems to us and is very unlikely to produce the results of peace and calm that we had envisioned it to provide. We might as well be calm, showing others the way rather than forcing it on them. And, when they choose not to take us seriously, then we can walk away. After all, it was meant to help. When it isn't needed anymore, no emotional contract binds us to it...save our own need to be heroic.

My advice is to find your heroism elsewhere.

Focus on creating a presence that draws others in and makes them desire to change—not because you're coercing them to, but because your presence alone provides healing. To do this, you would have to work on transforming your own being rather than forcing them to relinquish themselves and, sooner rather than later, they would be changed by your empathy, not force.

Building a Heart that Helps.

I get it. You've got your own issues. Why add the burden of caring for someone else to the things you've got to focus on?

Wait for a little. We were all made to be helpful, although admittedly, we sometimes are more apt to choose ourselves over every other person because it just seems like the 'smart' thing to do. Those who have achieved real transformation could only achieve that because they chose to look beyond themselves. At first, it might even seem counter-productive because, at the point where people need help, they are very unlikely to admit it. However, it can become something that guides our regular practice in life—if we actually allow ourselves to experience the totality of living.

And yes, there's always a reason to make use of such life-transformation skills. I believe the reason for which there's an upsurge in suicide rates is due to a lack of people who have imbibed helpfulness. This generation has bred a crop of selfish beings because of the focus on taking care of 'ourselves,' all while forgetting that if people around us, whom we love, are hurt, then we inevitably get hurt as well. As women, we have extraordinary capacities for empathy. We can put ourselves in the shoes of the other woman, picture her situation, and offer comfort to her. It is essential, especially when our loved ones feel overwhelmed by life states. And, as we take up the challenge to transform others, we are inevitably transformed as well.

However, to achieve this state of helpfulness, we must get rid of circumstances that prevent us from having loving hearts. Yes, in each of us are those barriers, which might have been formed as we were growing up—some of which were placed in us by our families or upbringing. Thus, we must be willing to change. It doesn't come easy; but I assure you, it's worth it.

People all over are broken. Sometimes, we want to help but are unable to because we don't have the mental capacities nor the emotional strength to do so. And so, we shy away and pretend that all is well when we are assured that 'nothing' is well. Some people find it in them to provide aid to loved ones. There are those people whom you find it easy to approach because you somehow know they can provide you with a healing presence. Healing simply radiates from them.

It is what we need the most today. Those who run to drugs, alcohol, sex and other such means of escape do so because they can't find a healing presence around them—for if they do, there would be no need to escape from the lives in which they live.

With this virtue, you can finally help in providing moral strength, spiritual prowess, and help them get through all forms of suffering without resorting to physical, mental, or emotional suicide. At the end of this exercise in helping people, your end goal is to aid those who have come in contact with you to regain their own probably 'lost' or 'buried' powers to heal. These features that a person has—ones that enable his or her presence in itself to provide healing—are usually seen as traits possessed in one's soul. When nurtured, it blossoms into something beautiful beyond measure. Effectively helping others requires that we have such a presence around us that encourages people, despite how stressed up they are.

I can, although, assure you that this process would involve painful and frustrating moments. It is worth it because it opens you up to yourself. Do you like to be tried? Most people don't. In fact, it is super stressful to learn patience, especially when you think you're helping people. It is a vulnerable process, both for you and the person you're in the process of helping. I do not de-emphasize the need for you to gain educational qualifications that are needed in the provision of assistance to other people; however, the distinguishing factor between two people with the same academic qualifications regarding the results they get is that one person has gone through the painful process of vulnerability, while the other one hasn't and thinks that solely by his or her qualification, appreciable progress can be made. So not true!

Did you just say, "Fine. I'd focus on building this vulnerability by myself"?

Well, don't because you can't do so without the input of the feelings of others. It isn't something that can be built in isolation; instead, it is an effect that happens when we allow our relationships to become all-encompassing and rich enough to bear our thoughts, feelings…and everything. You will notice if there's a gradual improvement in your ability to help others from the way people respond to you, rather than by thinking of the 'quality' of your own help.

Challenging the Helplessness into Which We Were All Born.

How have we accepted to wallow through life with our souls in shambles?

We must be able to live through fear and helplessness and come out on the other side of them. Before you come up with an excuse of being 'physically helpless,' the very truth is that physical helplessness cannot be equated with spiritual or psychosocial helplessness.

It's amazingly sad how much in bondage we can be to our emotions. It is similar to, if not deeper than, physical pain. People, from infants to adults, have withered away and died physically because they did not receive the love and care their spirits needed to blossom. It is a spectrum of responses, which eventually results in death after going through varying versions of depression.

NOTE: Feeling helpless is **NOT** the same as being objectively helpless. We must recognize the difference because our brains and emotions do not recognize this difference, thereby causing us to react in similar ways.

The truth is that beyond the surface and these versions of helplessness that appear to be life-sucking, are certain wrong beliefs about our own abilities to take care of scary situations in our lives, perhaps because of what culture has molded us to believe about ourselves, and so on.

A particularly inspiring example of how to rise above all forms of mental limitations that plunge us into helplessness is the story of Nelson Mandela who, despite being locked up in prison, still showed the world it was possible to be in control of one's mental and spiritual states—and to change the world, regardless of the hurdles we've got to surmount.

As you can survive and thrive in the midst of such challenging mental states yourself and, as such, come out of it wholly transformed, you can then hold other people by their hands and see them through such circumstances. You know that when a person comes to you for help, what it means is that they are yet to fully give up on surviving whatever situation has held them bound. If they truly had no hope, the wouldn't have come to us for help at all. Therefore, what is your role in this situation, you ask? Simple. It is to remind these people who are at high risk of giving up that there's more to life and living. It is to help them realize that although the fire in them is not stirred up, there is, indeed, still some leftover fire that can be fanned to flame. It is to help them gradually; slowly but surely, they can take over their own minds once again and think like people who are in control over their lives. We'd naturally titrate that depending on how severe or mild a life experience is, people would either collapse in them or shrug them off without as much as getting hurt—but how wrong!

Funny, but a life-threatening experience like a hurricane that wipes away one's entire family, as well as one's lifelong possessions, might bring one person near the brink of suicide, while to another person, it might just be the catalyst for releasing unbelievable excellence. This proves that it isn't the situation in itself that kills a man, but the reservoir of hope present in such an individual before the occurrence of such a debilitating circumstance. As a matter of fact, it is the little things that eventually break most people; not the hard, life-threatening ones. It is as though one has gotten to the end of the road and, once again, one more little, frustrating event pops its ugly head, and you say to yourself, "I can't take this anymore!" while shouting out of deserved exasperation.

We have to learn on our own that in life (as we are often not taught), severe emotions aren't to be shoved into the corner. They should, in fact, be welcomed as vital signs that we are alive! Granted, the rawness of these emotions might scare us, but without actually experiencing them, we are losing out on the beauty of our beings.

Moments of crisis actually birth for us strong growth. These moments of exploration into our beings are catalysts that turn us from helpless munchkins into powerful, broken beings. People are often terrified by their own discoveries of themselves and, instead of admitting this, it's easier to simply put your hand in your hair and claim confusion. Confusion is, in this way, an escape from the experience of overcoming your fears. Therefore, encourage the people in your corner—those women who seem to be unable to claim control over their own lives—to live through the confusion and open themselves up to see how they actually feel about things.

It is hard on us, as well. The one who is providing assistance and encouragement must be able to maintain a calm internal milieu, even when the person to be helped is going through a massive myriad of emotional overwhelm. You'd be surprised by how easy it is to get drained when people pour out all of the pent-up frustration on you. If this happens, it already forces you to withdraw some form of emotional support because you're merely in overdrive. And guess what? You might begin to act out.

Those radical, overreaching measures you take in trying to handle the feelings of others show that you have not fully come to terms with your own emotional intelligence. Therefore, of everything, you need to be able to help others adequately is the ability to remain comfortable with them expressing their emotions. As it stands, one very sad way by which we push others away and, in the process, further compound their problems, is reacting too steeply to their emotions. To be okay with the expression of strong emotions needs a lot of practice. In this way, we learn not to do something irrational or stupid in the presence of people who are experiencing some form of breakdown. By all means, no matter how you choose to look at it, whatever emotions people are going through provide the window to their souls.

You are not indispensable, but if you stay comfortable with the emotions of other people—irrespective of how 'dead' they feel—then you open them up to see how they can be comfortable with their own feelings. Through your eyes, they can, therefore, see that life is not over because, of course, you have learned to maintain your cool and not to act as though their lives were over. We must find that spot in our minds that provide us with soulful escape from being as overwhelmed as the people whom we try to give aid and healing to.

People in pain intuitively recognize the calmness, unfazed responses, and positive attitude which you provide them. These qualities are what allow them to finally gravitate towards us as people who are capable of providing help. For this exciting reason, you must be ready to find out about yourself—that 'thing' that helps you keep calm (not just on the exterior, but to maintain your calm deep within your being—not only for you, but majorly for the person looking at you intently, trying to see if you'd be judgmental or if you're able to take in their 'stuff' with much camaraderie.

What's your outlet? Picturing a calm stream as it overflows its banks? Speaking words to yourself that promote a nice aura?

Whatever it is, you'd notice that your 'outlet,' if it is effective, does not just provide help to your client or the sister in pain before you; it also helps you. It enlarges your heart, makes you more capable of giving, and ultimately builds your confidence in your ability to help or give. This is the major differentiating factor between those who sigh out of exasperation after having attempted to provide help and others who smile subtly in victory because they have been able to provide massive aid to other people. There's no point in being helpful if we only treat symptomatically, rather than getting to the root of the matter, right?

Often, at the root of hopelessness (which is felt so aptly by people) is the feeling that they have been detached from the support of 'friends and family' and every other support structure they're used to, at a point when they seem not to be able to handle life's crises really well. And being alone can drive anyone mad. Infants, when left alone without human contact and nurturing, will cry at first, attempting to draw attention towards themselves. After a while, these tears lead to hopelessness, and they are apt to give up—and die. Same goes for adults, with the difference being that we can verbalize what is happening in and around us and, as such, have the possibility of finding a solution to the matters ailing us.

The Blessing of Connectedness.

As much as we need to feel in charge and in control of our lives, one crucial need of humans is to be able to connect to, at least, some parts of other people's lives.

Right from the outset, key ways to bring prisoners down has always involved the use of emotional isolation (from everyone; other prisoners inclusive) as a technique—one which almost always works. Mental health issues have a strong background in how we feel at all times. For example, a psychotic patient who thinks people are following her and who's hearing voices instructing her to carry out certain tasks has probably felt controlled by people in the past—and this is now acting as one of the complications of burying the past.

It is important to know how active and awesome our minds are. For example, missing human links are often recreated by our minds and can be considered the onset of a mental health issue. Sadly, the only source of emotional respite might be those irregular, weird, and imaginary conversations being had with non-living individuals. To pull them out of this is not to act as though it is an emotional emergency. Instead, you need to be able to show them that you can love and be helpful. Open yourself up to be aware of how that person feels, instead of taking the regular, negating step of shutting out their pain in the hope that it doesn't ignite in you some sort of deep-seated pain you've been trying to ignore or forget. (This is why a lot of us are dissuaded from helping others. It simply reminds us too much of our own hurt.)

As impossibly plain as it sounds, the best thing you can do for anyone (regarding their emotional health) is to welcome them and make them feel like they are important in our world, and not just some inconvenience or something that requires saving from themselves. I tell you this: As women, there's nothing more sacred than knowing another woman views your life as revered and that you are particularly special in the eyes of this person. It releases you to express yourself, even in ways you haven't been able to do when only you are in the room! It's magical and probably accounts for why it is super rare as well.

This is what it means to truly love: **Accept people**.

We have often argued within ourselves when we see people we love 'sinking,' as we convince ourselves that, indeed, there's something we should be able to do to help out! Not so. Sometimes, all we've got to simply do is to 'be.' Sensitive people feel the most hurt, yet they know that if they lose this sensitivity, every part of themselves would be lost. They would inevitably lose that unique feature that makes them stand out of the pack. As a sensitive woman, do not attempt—no matter how tempted you are—to shut off the bulb of your sensitivity. I cannot overemphasize that **THIS**, more than anything else, is what makes you, **YOU!** The only way to stay joyful despite someone else's sorrow (and no, you aren't betraying them by being joyful; you are, in fact, preparing them for an emotional contagion with joy) is to recognize, see beyond the surface, and know that this mark of suffering is a mark of life. When we accept and maintain this feeling of joyfulness, even when other people are suffering, it increases our abilities to heal them, as well as ourselves. As such, we gain fresh perspectives and can become exciting and new healing beings.

Can you look at **EVERY** moment of your life as the happiest moment you've ever experienced? While this sounds like a distant possibility, it is often far from being the truth. How can you be happy when you have just experienced a major catastrophe? To what end is such befuddled joy?

What we can do is experience some forms of happiness, even in different moments, as they come. The beautiful thing is you can point to ways in which otherwise plain, everyday people exhibit acts of heroism. Caring for the sickly ones in our lives, seeing them become shadows of the people they once were; yet holding onto hope that they can make it through, and whatever the case may be, we would stand by them until the end.

Overcoming mental breakdowns and showing up like a boss to your life so that you can carry out your necessary duties; turning around from being a hostile person because of the abusive situations faced in earlier years, into becoming a loving, welcoming individual who chooses to see always see the best in others; standing up for the truth they know and that bugs them, when they could have been complacent and done nothing to change the narratives they see—all being forms of heroism.

As individual unsung heroes and heroines, there's only one thing that cuts short our heroic fingerprints to the outside world: While we might, indeed, be heroic about one thing, many of us are rarely heroic about everything we do. What might have zero effect on one person could be the life-changing negative force in another's life. Your greatest nemesis—that Achilles heel of yours—is another's strength!

Although we are similar in that each of us is born to see helplessness and fear, the activator of these emotions in us is as different from one person to the other, just as light is from the day. This further corroborates the truth that the person you intend to help might quite be capable of dealing with their current life stressor, even if it seems like a dire emergency to you! That is why the best step to take is to calm down, take in their energies without allowing it to overstimulate you, and have at the back of your mind that, indeed, they are capable of dealing with whatever stressful situation is all around them.

Self-evaluation is key in this process. Hence, you cannot afford to—as a provider of help in these circumstances—deny your own shortfalls or allow yourself to be seen as the all-in-all help for those you love. You aren't flawless. In the first place, that's what enables you to provide such keen help! When you discover that you're unable to, for some intrinsic limiting reason, provide help anymore, kindly show them the way to another source of help. Don't act as though they are the reason for your 'breakdown.' Don't turn it around to make them feel more vulnerable than they are currently.

If you're the one in need of help, my lady, don't feel sad if it feels like you are moving around several people, all in a bid to find the help you need. Something isn't 'wrong with you' for needing mental connection. Perhaps the people you've met along the journey of needed help are reminded of other people who've hurt them in the past by you, which might incapacitate them from actually giving you the needed help. It doesn't mean you're damaged; it could just be that you guys aren't mentally compatible! More than anything else, it could be that your issues remind them of their own problems, making them unable to help you. At that moment, they may be ill-equipped. Don't sweat it.

The woman who's trying to help must know that to all people, she cannot be all things. Admitting that you're not a superhero is, in fact, a sign that you're made for the superhero life. Nonetheless, we can still be supportive. The art of helpfulness requires that we can all the time bring to life a loving nature towards people around us. This requires that we are okay with the emotions we have to observe others express before us, as well as those emotions which well up within us as others express theirs. Harder than it sounds, this ability to let others flow without getting overwhelmed to the point we are seemingly also helpless might tempt us to do something drastic because the situation before us seems like such an emergency. The proof of our strength is the ability to remain calm, extend our hands in support and loyalty, and keep that welcoming spirit alive.

While in emotionally overwhelming situations, it does us well to remember that every one of us has been born in a state of helplessness. The helper strengthens her ability to nurture her healing power and presence, especially if she can keep going when it gets hard, and she has to be more vulnerable than she planned.

NOTE: Emotional crises shouldn't be treated the same as when someone comes into the emergency room with multiple organ injuries and requires several different doctors to help save this life from what appears to almost be a lost battle.

Instead, crises can be turned around on their heads to become opportunities for creative excellence. How, you ask?

The Solution.

To be aware of how humiliated we've ever felt, all we need is to be in constant touch with our humanity. Certainly, we have all gone through miry, difficult situations—ones so hard, they make us feel like quitting on life. Emotional pain can have intensely shearing effects on our hearts. We have all experienced some degree of irrational behavior; hence, we are capable of sympathizing with others when they are somewhat irrational, illogical, or unreasonable. The temptation to be irresponsible has gotten a hold of many of us, enough to see how that can make other people feel. If we choose to remain honest to ourselves, we'd see that other people aren't so different from us. As such, we emphasize openness and shun the act of condemning others.

Other people don't need you to endorse their feelings of helplessness, which is what you do when you give an emergency an emotionally-packed response or action. Can you take the emotional imbalances of others in stride, while remaining the healing figure you've always been? That'd be superb!

Another way of handling such an emotional emergency is by seeing it as something which will, overall, yield interesting returns for you and the persons involved. They are, indeed, exceptional opportunities granted us: to be able to look into the hearts of others while we look into ours as well. It might have begun as a crisis that was avoided at all cost at the beginning, but it can end up being that reason for which we are forever grateful. Life is never black and white. Pain often opens our eyes to pure realities we never thought existed.

It is fulfilling, indeed, on that day when you get to see how an emotional emergency has brought about newer, fresher opportunities for your growth, as well as that of other people. Also, witnessing how it has empowered the one who's deep into the crisis to see that life situations can be handled, no matter how pressing they seem to us. It is probably still the only means through which a person can confront that which stares them in the face and threatens that they wouldn't live through yet another day to deal with their inclinations towards being helpless, so they end up seeing it as enriching opportunities. Isn't it exciting when someone who felt helpless can now provide healing to another person? Giving help to and bringing another woman out of the rut makes you 'that lady' who is building ladders for the next generation of phenomenal, transformative, total women in your community and beyond.

You are that person who helps a fellow woman get over the hurt of her childhood that has reared its ugly head once again through a life situation, and you are creating a work of genius! You make them better people to work with as more loving mates and spouses, and more effective parents. In effect, you change the world in your own little way, one step at a time!

What better way to show your strength as a boss woman than being super helpful! Go rock the world, superwoman!

Chapter 5

MAKING BOSS MOVES IN CHALLENGING TIMES

And Propelling Yourself Towards the Achievement of Your Purpose and Passion

Carlene Randolph

The rule of success is never to give up, and one day, you'd top the charts!

I know firsthand how easy it is to give up, especially after getting repeated rejections in life, relationships, and at work. After that, you're all spent!

Maybe you've just been fired from a job you held so much in esteem—one which you gave all your hours to for years and years and believed you'd retire from—but you've been literally thrown out into the cold to fend for yourself. You might have lost the confidence and charisma you had when you first started working there. The zeal for it has all but reduced to zero as you recalibrated your priorities in life. Now, you're in a mess because you feel stuck on a spot and no one seems to be coming to your rescue, no matter how you internally scream out in pain. Even if you're pretending that all's well, one look at you, and I can tell not all is well.

So, let's change the narrative regarding career excellence now, shall we?

The world is rapidly changing regarding the kind of qualifications you need to succeed. Heck: Apple, Inc., Google, and a couple of big companies have already scrapped off their list the need to have a college degree to work with them! If all you've know all your life is a one-way street, the current way of doing things will mentally stress you out and throw you off-balance. You'd end up so confused, there wouldn't be any rational way out of the mental quagmire you'd find yourself in.

Total B...

Not too long ago, the only thing you required as a successful employee or employee-to-be was competence in a particular craft. Go to school, gain some sort of competence and, alongside your qualifications, you were home and dry. In today's world, that's a recipe for falling on your butt. There are millions of 'degreed,' multiple-qualified, competent professionals out there. If you've got nothing new, dynamic, and creative to bring to the table, you wouldn't have any relevance in any industry in which you find yourself.

The ages between 35-55 are challenging because you're shuffling between health issues, sending off kids to college, empty-nest syndrome, thinking of how to spice up your marital life, and so on. Your mind is unlikely to remain on one spot, making concentration an arduous, almost impossible task. How, then, can you offer something so strong that the world of business would choose you over a youngster who's brimming with so much energy?

I'll tell you how.

Here's a quote by Tom Peters: "We are CEOs of our own companies: Me, Inc. To be in business today, our most important job is to be head marketer for the brand called 'You.'"

Your brand is you. This couldn't be truer at this stage of your life when you've gained significant wisdom due to situations you've faced, conquered, and come through on the other side. Therefore, what you need is:

- To have the right kind of people noticing you for the quality of services you can render.
- To have this set of people respond to you swiftly when you reach out to them.
- To improve your online and offline presence (in the right quarters) so that this set of people (who can be of great benefit to you) don't overlook you and also reach out to you.
- For this exceptional group of life-changers to bypass other people and choose you because they recognize that what you offer is, indeed, unique.
- Of course, to have clients who are ready to pay a premium for your exceptional top-notch services.
- And also, they must be loyal to you and be so proud of your work's quality, they send referrals your way.

The thing is that with personal branding, even when you are out of a job because of things such as 'downsizing' or the road gets really rough and you need a way out, you can leverage on the wisdom and skills you've acquired over the years to position yourself such that you can never be the one to lose out! And if you get fired? Well, they've only given you ample time to grow your brand into one that's forever unforgettable!

Here are a few steps to help you build your brand and keep you fulfilled on the path you've chosen:

STEP 1: Have a target audience.

Once you've decided on what you want your brand to be about, on the things that shake you to your core and which you cannot do without (i.e., once you are honest enough to recognize your passion—even if it isn't your current line of work), you can then proceed to focus on a particular audience.

Don't be so excited that you begin to send out your newly-packaged resume to all the people on your contact list. You might be setting yourself up for disappointment if you choose to go along this path. In fact, you might be pushing people away by sending messages that look like spam to them, just because you have finally identified and are ready to pursue your passion. Don't do that. Acting desperate is never a good thing.

I want to ensure you never become the person for whom "I'll get back to you" becomes the principal response you get from people all over. You could be doing way better!

You deserve to be seen for the excellent brand that you are. Excellent brands aren't known for dire acts of desperation; they are known for keeping their cool and addressing target audiences with marked precision and accuracy. Therefore, you must pick out the demographics of your target audience and approach them with dead-set precision, aimed at getting positive responses.

NOTE: Not everyone will be your client. Fish out the demographics of those who are capable of hiring you, and then approach them.

That being said, you need to act precisely. That comes by way of **networking** with people within your target demographic. It is important not to ignore your own inner circle and then begin to fraternize with people outside that circle. Thinking wrongly that people within your circle do not possess anything that could be of help to your new emerging brand will prove damaging from the start. You'd be surprised at how some friends will push for you and bring you to the limelight with their incessant faith in your brand. There is always at least one person within your inner circle who can provide you with the solutions to the problems you're going through.

After leveraging on those friends, you then move on to beyond your network and find people outside of it who can either make a referral for you to the right people or guide you.

STEP 2: Request guidance, not a job.

The right kind of people—those with life-changing relationships and endless opportunities—didn't get there by merely requesting jobs. They have mentors and role models. In short, they do not lack guidance. That is why, as soon as you get your foot in the door by establishing contact with key individuals within your target audience, it would be destructive to start pestering them with job requests. Instead, request guidance and keep on building and blossoming strong relationships.

Tell them how amazed you are by the work they do and their impact/relevance to society, as you ask them to provide some insight into how you can also stay relevant in your niche. If they see you are interested in true growth, many of them would be willing to hold your hand and show you the way. Of course, in the process, you'd meet with life-changing opportunities that will open your eyes and mind. They are far more beneficial than just touting mere jobs!

Before taking the time to craft messages to these key players within your target audience, do well to:

- Go through their social media profiles. These days, you can find interesting snippets of people's lives and find out their general mien about life based on most of their posts. Do well to go through their profiles, and you'd find interesting ways to bring up conversations with them.
- Knowing their interests, conduct in-depth research on their background—educational and otherwise—to find out the reason for their life interests. Get yourself up-to-date about this. It helps to form a smooth, sleek connection with them.
- Finally, connect with them on common grounds. There would be some things about them that resonate deeply with you. Let your passion shine through your conversations with them and watch as you light up the room with them, even if you're communicating over social media!

Now that you have opened up the floor for genuine, interesting, and life-changing conversation, you can then steer the direction of conversation towards your goal (you might have even stimulated them enough to suggest to you what you best need at that point)! At this stage, you should have put down people-pleasing, over-flattering tendencies. At the top isn't exactly a beloved trait. Therefore, as you approach your target audience, be smart enough to compliment them without being pushy or acting like they are your 'salvation.' You are coming to them with a solution-providing mindset; not as someone who's only out to receive and not give anything beneficial in return!

STEP 3: Show how much of an expert you are.

Life's blows might have made you less confident of your abilities, but it pays no one when you downplay the amount of excellence you can bring to the table and, in the process, allow other less-competent and excellent people take the spotlight instead of you. You might have learned always to second-guess yourself, but playing small has never really helped anyone, has it?

Therefore, introduce yourself as an expert—not because you want to impersonate anyone, but because, my darling, an expert is who you are!

When experts talk, people listen. When novices speak, people might listen—or they might not, depending on how motivated they are. Another cool thing about being an expert is that you get paid for being able to simply shed light on grey areas and provide insight. Believe me when I say: You are wise. You cannot have spent so many years going through and coming out of challenging times without building wisdom and spilling it out every chance you get to speak.

You have, in effect, become the kind of person who can push others towards fewer losses and more gains in life. Therefore, your prospective clients should know this about you. Your years of experiencing failures have taught you where not to head and, as such, you can guide them appropriately.

Show them you are an expert. Ways of achieving this have become much easier because of the myriad of online opportunities availed to us to share our expertise. Some of these ways include:

- Owning a personal blog. I don't know how you feel about blogging. You might think of it as cheesy child's play, or it might have been an inspiring concept to you in the past. One sure thing I know about blogging is its ability to shoot you to the limelight if you have something to say that people want to hear. Also, consistency is key. As an expert, share loads of your expertise on your blog consistently. Share the posts with members of your target audience and effectively convince them of the fact that you are capable of being an asset to them.
- Make use of the power of storytelling. If you're convinced about your passion, the words will come. Even if you aren't a writer, speak about it into a recording device or make a video about what you think can be improved in your line of work. Next, share that critical piece of information with your

target audience using stories! Always remember that as humans, we connect more readily to stories because we can put ourselves in the position of the protagonist (and whoever else the story makes mention of), stirring our emotions in the process. Don't be surprised if, after a grueling, interesting storytelling session, you have people sending you hundreds of emails to see how you can be of assistance to them!

Step 4: Make it your sole desire to help your prospects win!

This is the point where I like to see you as someone on a mission to save the people you claim to care about; those whom you have interest in providing service to.

Even before you get one client, it should be your daily mantra to provide such excellent service, they would **ALWAYS** stand out and win, irrespective of how stiff the competition is.

As Zig Ziglar once said, *"You can have everything you want if you will just help other people get what they want."* Quite easy!

As soon as you can identify the needs of your target audience, the next step is to help them get it. Even if you aren't the best fit for a job, you can connect them to someone in the circle who is and, in the process, form a lasting relationship with them on the basis of trust and mutual support for each other. Go the extra mile by sharing worthy, clickable content with those in your target audience and space. You might notice that soon enough, it stops being one-sided and they also start to share stuff with you! The lesson here is that help often begets help.

To make it an even more personal gesture, send them private messages as well while sending them helpful content. You can frame the message to look something like this:

"I thought this article would be helpful to you because of 'x, y, and z'..."

Simply make it personal enough for them to feel included in your thoughts and for them to know that you actually care about maintaining the relationship you've built with them, and not just because of the favors you intend to get from them. Soon enough, they'll see you in the light you're creating about yourself, instead of as an opportunist that has come within their space to take away from them yet again.

Conclusively, you needn't see giving up as an option. Every day, we fight the same battle over and over until we conquer. See yourself as the persistent stonecutter who chooses to keep hitting on a single spot, irrespective of the fact that little progress seems to be made over the time effort is being expended. Always know that the fact that progress doesn't seem evident doesn't mean none is being made.

Carlene Randolph

As long as you keep hitting on that spot and refuse to move an inch or give up in surrender, you will see the change you see.

The key word here remains 'consistency.'

Chapter 6

EMBRACING THE POWER TO STEP BACK FROM TOXICITY

It Lies in You

Carlene Randolph

Toxicity is like that weed that grows on a lush piece of farmland and, in no time, oversteps its bounds until it takes over the entire farmland.

Toxicity breeds anger, malice, fear, doubt, and ultimately, it crushes you until you're made to surrender to its ugly fangs. It can come in the form of events or shaped like people. We are often seemingly naïve when the toxic process is implanted in our minds, and before you say "Jack Robinson," you have become the bitter fellow you swore to avoid.

I have heard many a time that women are bitter, angry, foul-word-spewing "bitches" who are so angry at life (and men), they would do anything to project this seething anger within them. As a middle-aged woman, it is likely you have been described as 'bitter' if you let your emotions run your life because these emotions of ours...how so lush! In those moments, we often forget that we have the choice to either be bitter or maintain calmness, both on the exterior and deep within our souls.

If it is a saddening event that has occurred (e.g., a divorce), it is very easy to tie your stagnation in other parts of your life to that even. It is a common human error to relate one's progress (or lack thereof) to specific events. In doing so, we forget one very crucial fact: Events happen universally. No one is an 'island' of negative events. They come and go, with none of them being inherently good or bad. You cannot take one event and make it account for all of your life's problems. Neither can you assume that because one event brought one woman to her knees, it will inevitably bring you to yours.

Total B...

In the last two chapters, I have tried to bring a change to your mindset and to help you know that what completely destroys one person just might be the catalyst for your own uplifting. You would be a smart person to take an event, magnify it, and see through it to find out those immense benefits that you can accrue from them, even when they are unfavorable.

Toxicity is something you can choose to either embrace or walk away from. Very few people are smart enough to walk away from toxic situations. The majority of individuals bathe themselves in these situations and even refuse to grow out of them.

The test of events is one which many of us fail. Sadly, it is often what determines who moves on to the next level and who remains on the same spot. This is why it takes a special chapter in this book. When something doesn't go as expected in your life, do you turn to resentment against other people perceived to have a hand in your sorrow, or do you intentionally choose to find the benefits of whatever it is that disturbs you so much? You cannot control events; why beat yourself up over them? Why build up brick walls of resentment in your heart over things that were programmed to break you? Why do you want to give anyone the satisfaction of seeing you in a broken state?

Paralympics are doing great things for their countries, but think about it: They could have entertained toxic mindsets that make them feel as though they wouldn't amount to anything in life because they lack limbs!

Carlene Randolph

Some of the most heart-rendering musicians of all time were born blind, yet with their souls, they were able to touch what the sighted couldn't reach.

Terrible events in themselves hold no value. What do you choose to do with them? They are intensely powerful in shaping the trajectory of your life.

I speak so passionately about this because I have learned how much events can either make or mar a person using my personal experiences. From romantic to work relationships, I have had numerous reasons and opportunities to be bitter. I must admit that sometimes, I allow myself to wallow in unhealthy toxic mindsets and states. Never have I achieved anything beneficial because I allowed myself to be toxic. Instead, the only times I gained maximally from events were when I chose to see beyond the pain gripping my heart so tightly in moments when toxicity rears its ugly head and choosing to go forward in spite of it all.

And so, when I look into the eyes of other women, it is easy for me to see how badly they have been hurt and how much they hold on to such damage to their tender hearts—and why it seems like they are stuck on the same spot. It will be my undoing if I do nothing to help them see the beauty that is womanhood that is in them. To help them see the fact that they can feel so deeply shouldn't be the bane of their existence! It is a blessing; one which should be jealously guarded against the root of bitterness and toxicity that is thrown at us in our everyday lives.

Total B...

It is best to learn not to run away from failure or even pain, but to walk into every situation breezing through every event with your head held high. Pull out every toxic thought from your mind as you would eagerly pull a weed out of your beautifully crowded farmland. (I know how difficult this is because even as I pen this chapter, I am battling with events that attempt to place my mind on the toxic landscape.) In so doing, you are opening yourself up for massive progress. In every situation you are faced with, there's an opportunity for growth, increase, and largesse.

Chapter 7

EMBRACING POSITIVE PEOPLE INTO YOUR SPACE

"You attract into your life, the people who are reflections of yourself. Who are you attracting into your life?"

Total B...

The beauty of life is that even though you get moments of solitude, you cannot really live in isolation. At least that is true for most of us. Like you may have noticed, certain people are more comfortable hanging around you than others, and vice-versa. This is a function of the vibes emitted by yourself and such individuals. Ultimately, you will attract people who are synchrony with your personality on the inside.

What Crowd Are You Attracting?

The saying "Show me your friend and I'll tell you who you are" couldn't have been communicated any better. If you don't like the set of friends you currently have, instead of changing them, how about you ask what attracted you to them and them to you in the first instance? That's it! Once again, the Law of Attraction pops up! Something has to have bound you together in the first place, and it certainly wasn't bonding glue!

Therefore, if you aren't pleased with your set of friends, do something about it. Ask yourself deep, very truthful questions about their vices. Are you also a participant in those vices and is that what drew you to each other like magnetic forces?

The same goes for attracting certain excellent people into your life. This can only be possible if you have certain qualities in your life as excellent, positive individuals are very careful about their inner circle—just as you should be. In fact, to attract a lot of greatness into your life, one aspect of your life which you should be very careful about is who gains access to you and how frequently. You should never be too nice to limit access by a particular individual into your life. Be as sincere as possible in ensuring the people around you aren't limiters, but those who are excellent through and through.

Your Ideal Inner Circle.

The Law of Attraction is bigger than any single one of us. Just imagine a gathering of people—bosses in their own rights and people whom success is attracted to on so many fronts who lay out a plan for success. You will observe that within the space of only a short period, more ideas would have come up to achieve it and, before the gathering disperses, the plan may be well on its way to being actualized.

Take this same plan and give it to a group of naysayers. Right there and then, because they only keep on attracting failure into their lives, you will watch as that plan is shredded into bits and unrecognizable reasons for which it cannot be actualized.

In both scenarios, what was different? It definitely was the people! In other words, if, as a group, the major Law of Attraction at work in that group is negative, then even if one of them is positively-inclined, that one person might be unable to pull the whole group into a positive mental state and might end up decamping to the group of the negatively-inclined.

That is why your inner circle is important. Who are those who form the critical portion of your group of friends? If they are not individuals who are attracted to positivity, then you should rest assured the positive things which you attract aren't likely to last for long because they would lack the sustenance that could have been provided by a positively-inclined group of individuals.

Changing You on the Inside.

The key to having the right kind of people surrounding you is very much dependent on whom you really are on the inside. It's easy to project an image that isn't true about yourself, but eventually, you would let your guard down and show forth your true personality.

Instead of spending so much time creating all those multiple walls to protect your real person, how about opening up to yourself and discovering whom you are to find out what needs to be changed? If that is settled, it might not be such a difficult thing to change your circle of friends. In fact, the wrong circle wouldn't be comfortable hanging around the right you!

Chapter 8

EMBRACING YOU: BEING ALL YOU CAN BE

"When you look into the mirror, what do you see?"

Total B...

I know you intend to build for your life a lasting legacy. You have begun to ask questions such as, "What will come out of my life? What will be the result of my life? When I leave the earth, what will be said of me?"

Sometimes, we run away from looking at our own reflections because it speaks volumes about what we are, where we are, and where we're headed in life. It's easier to ignore those salient points in our lives because it can be difficult to face them square on. Besides, whatever you need to distract you is ever-present. Just name your distraction, and I assure you that it'd emerge from whatever crevice it is hidden.

Nonetheless, it is wise to evaluate your life every once in a while, to ascertain if you're making progress or if you must intensify your efforts in a given direction. What if you need to make a U-turn if you must fulfill your purpose? All of these require wisdom.

You must always be aware of the current state of things in your life because it conditions you to implement changes that would make you soar from the current position you are in. Self-evaluation is key because it forces you to think about what you have been attracting into your life; the events, circumstances, and people that have encircles you over the last couple of years. The truth is, whatever surrounds us is a direct reflection of our frame of minds at any given time.

Do lack and doubt surround you? Then there's something that needs to be tweaked in your mindset because lack and doubt are coming from there.

So, let's do a simple exercise: Take a look at yourself in a full-length mirror. Enjoy the view. Take in your beauty—the curves, the finesse, and the features you love the most about your body.

Next, look into your eyes via the mirror. Make eye contact with yourself. Keep staring for the next 10 minutes and refuse the urge to take your eyes away from the view. (Here's why you might be tempted to look elsewhere: Thoughts might begin to flood your mind about yourself; your body, your work, your personality, what people think of you, your body (once again), how your face and hair look, and how other parts of your body look.) For as long as possible, keep your eyes on that image of yourself. Then, stop.

For many individuals, this exercise would probably not last five minutes before they get irritated, to the point of nausea. Most of the time, this nausea isn't birthed from their body's frame. Even those with the best body forms and shapes in this world aren't exempt from these nauseous states on visualizing their own images.

I suppose you're wondering why this is so. Why are people so scared to look at the 'real' or true reflections of themselves? Why are they prone to look away as soon as they can? The sad reality is that what most people see about themselves is negativity, which are thoughts capable of stirring up deep-seated nausea.

Now, we are getting to an action point—the hard part of this imagery. I would like you to write down every single thing you have mirrored about yourself. It will help you know your starting point. What have you attracted into your life up until now? I know it's quite hard to look yourself in the eye and be honest about what you have succeeded in attracting into your life or about the situation in which you currently find yourself, especially if you have made some really bad experiences in life. However, you cannot move forward until you know where your current position is. That is the first step in the direction of progress.

Why Do You Keep Attracting the Same Things 'Unknowingly'?

It is quite alarming to a lot of people that no matter how hard they try or refuse to try to attract certain things, events, or people into their lives. Those are the very same things, events, or people that seem to be attracted into their lives. When this situation is mired in negativity (as it often is), these individuals are tempted to ask (often out of frustration), "Why is this so?" Moreso, there is this certainty that in no way are they desiring those negative circumstances show up in their lives; yet, it is as if these circumstances are occurring in sequence and are uncalled for.

Let me discuss a shocking revelation: The more you see something happening in your environment, the more you are configured to expect such happenings! You don't even have to desire it consciously; it only has to be before you, and voila! It is replicated in your own life, without permission...multiple times.

For instance, someone who is in need consistently has spotted lack in his environment. That is precisely what he begins to create a vibe for. This vibe then brings in more lack; more need into his life. The revealing thing about this concept is that it is independent of desire or purpose.

It has been noticed that when someone who is a native of what is known as a 'third-world country' is in his or her own country and visualizes laws being broken and nothing being done to punish the breaking of such law or that there is no intact system of retributive justice in place, this person is likely to begin to break those same laws—without even ruminating on it. What has happened is that by merely spotting this loophole and seeing others perpetrating those acts, there is a strong vibe being sent out to be a part of the act(s).

Let us take that same individual and place them in an environment with an active system of retributive justice for a period of time. Watch as this same individual complies with all of the laws and rules of that country without having any issues with the system. Also, what has happened is that a positive vibe instead of obeying the rules of this country has been put in place, and this individual follows suit.

This tells us something fundamental about what we choose to place before our eyes on a daily basis: Without knowing it, we conform to the image of that which we see. This has been exploited by the advertising agencies, as they only have to advertise certain things during TV hours during commercial breaks. You, the potential consumer, only has to see the product being advertised a couple of times. You watch as the box of pizza is ordered, delivered, opened, and then a yummy bite is taken and munched along with a cold drink. After a while, you are likely to order your own box of pizza! You see, a positive vibe of enjoyment has been sent out. Since you also want to experience that same positive vibe, you do the same thing: order your own box of pizza!

"Do My Words Attract Excellence or Sub-Excellence?"

What words are you speaking to yourself?

Words aren't just mere sayings; they carry power. What we say goes a long way in predicting the outcome of our lives—every minute fragment of it. Our vibes are determined by our words, whether spoken, typed, or in any other format. Simply put, our words are our life, which is why the Law of Confession is a vital component of the Law of Attraction.

While the word 'hospital' probably connotes a negative vibe for most people, it might not necessarily be so for the surgeon who is about to pull on some really innovative surgery that could be life-changing! And so, we see that the same words can have completely different meanings to different individuals.

However, some words have exactly the same effect on all individuals (or almost all individuals), and a few of these words would be addressed in the subsequent portion of this chapter.

1. DON'T

The word 'don't' can seem like a harmless instruction-like word. **DON'T** go over there. **DON'T** be a cry-baby. **DON'T** sleep over at his house. **DON'T** come back here.

Without a doubt, 'don't' is a strongly negative word. It carries such strength and, when spoken with a little bit of persuasion, can be a powerful tool in the arsenal of the individual who's using it. However, there's something fundamentally wrong with the use of such strong, negative words such as 'don't' and 'not.' It is that whatever the thing you are requesting not to be done, the recipient of the instruction has to first of all form an image of doing that thing and then consciously decide not to do it. As you might guess, their efforts might not be enough to stop them from carrying out the task.

Therefore, consistent use of the word 'don't' often results in an equivalent desire to perform the task or, at least, 'taste the forbidden fruit.'

2. STOP

The problem with this word is that it sounds like an order is being given and, well, very few people like taking orders. Quite akin to the first word on this list, consistent use of this word isn't likely to achieve the much-desired change. If you keep telling yourself to 'stop' doing a particular thing, you just might find out that efforts are intensified towards performing that act—and you fall flat on your face! The same thing can be said if you keep asking someone to stop doing something: You just might find the person doubles his or her efforts to disobey your order.

As a matter of fact, the Law of Attraction is just like you and I hearing what we have been asked not to hear while filtering the word 'don't' out of a statement.

How about we find a solution to this by resetting our minds to do better? Instead of making use of the word 'don't,' how about you state what you 'do' want?

Amazingly, when we do this, we change our vibes and are bound to have new results. The good this is, like I said earlier, these vibes can either be good or bad—but not both at the same time. So, with this, you would be sending out only the good, positive vibes, as opposed to the negative ones.

Consistency in the Use of the Law of Confession.

The Law of Confession is only as applicable as the consistency of its use. The most successful people in this world know how to make the best possible use of this law while, of course, the mediocre use of it—howbeit to their own disarray in life and business.

At a conference I attended recently, one of the chief speakers, on mounting the podium, had, as one of his opening statements, the words: "I keep to time." The amazing thing was that he kept to time. To me, that wasn't really the big deal. What I observed was that about 8-10 times during his one-hour presentation, he repeated those same words, almost at an average of a 10-minute interval. He didn't only keep to time; he finished his presentation before the allotted time was up, and yet, it was a mind-blowing success!

While making positive confessions such as, "I am excellent. Only good things are drawn into my life today!" you might discover that along the way, some 'not so good' scenarios may rear their heads. What do you do during such situations? You cannot afford to change your confessions. Many people do not know that the energy they had invested in making positive confessions was lost simply because they didn't use the opportunity presented to them by what they considered to be a negative situation in the right manner. Therefore, what do you do?

Understanding the Power of Silence.

Silence can be a powerful tool, even when making use of the Law of Confession. The first thing you must know is what would help you in utilizing this very powerful tool: **YOUR WORDS MAKE YOU!** If you don't choose to be in control over the things which you say on a daily basis, you are choosing to let your life be run by outward circumstances, instead of running your life by yourself. Sadly, a lot of people would rather let circumstances run their lives, rather than be proactive about choosing to speak only the right words. But you aren't one of them; you are a subset of that proactive group which values excellent speech!

I wouldn't deny that there are some moments when, if you open your mouth to speak, all that would come out through your lips cannot be positive. You are confident that during this period, speaking is almost equivalent to lighting a match of fury and using it to set the paper on fire. Vividly imagine how much damage that would do if this piece of paper was placed in a pile of several other pieces of paper, several meters high. How much fire would emanate? Yes, there are those moments. Rather than viewing those moments as inevitable moments of destruction, you need to start seeing them as makers of destiny.

These moments would determine how far you would go in life and the speed of your rise. In those inevitable moments, the best, most-trusted thing to do is to keep silent. There is a Law of Confessional attraction which says that whatever you say would come to you. Instead of calling your child "stupid" or saying that he is a failure, keep quiet. Instead of marching to your boss' office in a fury and giving her a 'piece of your mind'—a piece that could wreck your entire career—keep quiet. Instead of shouting at your wife or even your girlfriend, causing great harm to your marriage or relationship, keep quiet.

Confess to Yourself.

One beautiful thing about the Law of Confession is that, even though we predominantly speak to others, we can still effectively speak to ourselves. It is said that with our outer ears, we listen to other people, but with our inner ears, we listen to ourselves. You are the only one who can speak life to yourself in the most predominant manner. This works, even if all you hear in your environment is negative.

Every single day, you need to ensure that making positive confessions are your default mode. Speak life into yourself, your health, your business, and your family. Confess that you are beautiful, and do so with such earnest and consistency that you believe it without a shadow of a doubt. Soon enough, others would believe it, too!

The Law of Attraction is such that it draws whatever you say in your direction! It is such a relevant law, no one can adequately function in life or become all that he or she was created to be—without putting it to good use and creating such immense energy within themselves—that the speech of others makes no significant impact on how they view themselves.

How Not to Absorb the Negative Confessions of Others.

For quite a number of individuals, the speeches of others have done more harm than good. These words, probably spoken by someone who was held in high regard, have created such a stronghold upon their minds that they have ruminated upon it over and over again until it became real to them and began carrying a life of their own.

In effect, these words were so deeply-absorbed that they now dwell within the crevices of their hearts and have formed insecurities within the minds of these persons. These persons are probably you and I, for we all have had people whom we hold in high esteem tell us off, and even unknowingly, left us to wither away. And withered, we have.

Today, I write not as someone who hasn't experienced the feelings of doubt and fear created by the negative speeches of others; I write as someone who has stood in those same steps and been mired in grief so great because I believed something terrible that was spoken over my life. However, it was unnecessary. After several years, I would discover that with my own words, I can easily reverse the wrong spoken over my life. With my own words, I would then speak greatness into my life. Here's how: I would convert the negative energy created by those words and transform the energy into a positive vibe that I can make use of for my own progress.

Instead of hearing "You have failed in life," I began to train my ears to hear the words, "You have succeeded in life!"

Speak in Past-Tense.

The Law of Confession works even better if you make those confessions as though they are already working in your life.

For instance, instead of saying "I will get that business deal," you can say "I *have gotten* that business deal." This way, you get the feeling of having experienced that feeling, and then you attract it with even much greater force than ever before!

Your New Default Mode.

It's pretty easy to locate what mode you are operating from and what your current vibe is. I say it's easy because your feelings are intrinsic. You live with them, and they are the true reflectors of your vibe. If you are down and feel really lonely or not quite happy, then it is almost certain your vibe is negative. If the opposite is true, you feel upbeat, and then your vibe is currently high. We need not conduct any tests to certify any of these.

The truth about the Law of Attraction, which makes it subject to change, is that it operates in the present without paying attention to what your vibe was just a few days, weeks, or months ago—or even a few minutes ago. What you reflect as your vibe is a current determination of your feelings and vice-versa. No carry-overs here! And so, it would repay you in the same coin as whatever vibe you are reflecting now.

Work on embracing only positive things into your being—accepting your flaws and all—and see how these loving tendencies translate into great excellence in all aspects of your life.

Chapter 9

EMBRACING CONTINUAL EXCELLENCE

"What can I attempt tomorrow that would make my success of today pale in comparison?"

Focus: *Attracting Continual Success.*

Some things are routinely attributed to bad luck. Here are just a few of them:

- A person who succeeds initially in business but after a while, that business plummets and hits rock bottom.
- A couple who has to visit the divorce court after 14 years of relatively blissful marriage.
- An unfortunate accident happens just a few miles from home on the day this young chap graduates from college.

"These things cannot be avoided," we are tempted to say with a depth of conviction. It is easy to give up before starting if you feel as though starting puts you at risk of embarrassing failure—especially if you have seen previously successful persons crumble and then think of how you would manage to remain successful after a couple of years down that same path. "Would I be able to make it safely home?" you ask yourself.

Someone once said that achieving success isn't the problem; not as much as maintaining that success.

Astonishingly, some individuals have been able to maintain success for decades! Some brands have been able to deliver top-notch quality for their brands over the years, and it isn't because their intelligence quotients are way above those of other people within the populace. No, not so at all! It is hard to find such people and brands, but they are out there! Kentucky Fried Chicken (KFC) is a classic example.

I have only been alive for a few years, but have watched people and corporations crumble after only a few years. I feel deeply terrible when I see such occurrences, yet within these few years, I have also seen people rise from the grassroots and achieve unparalleled success in their fields, become great, and never go back to their humble beginnings.

What was the difference? If you gave all of these scenarios only a glance, you would probably attribute these findings to luck: good luck for those who have succeeded, and bad luck for those who didn't make it to the finish line.

The Success of Today is the Mediocrity of Tomorrow.

When people celebrate success lavishly, many of them fail to remind themselves that the feeling of having succeeded is only transient. It passes. To keep on having this feeling as a constant part of one's daily life, you would have to do one of the following: either keep on reminding yourself of that successful venture or achieve more success.

Which looks more like a vital option for you? I hope it's the latter because that definitely gives me goosebumps!

Staying in the past and reveling on its accomplishments is only proof that you don't believe you can do better in the future. It is proof that you probably feel as though you stumbled upon greatness and that you cannot reproduce it or create something better. This is the root of stagnancy.

One of the common things about really successful individuals is that they never really stop at just one level of success. Their exploits go on and on, and they keep on improving. There is no sense of having done that which is impossible to beat. If anything, they are always one step ahead of the pack because they are convinced that there is room for improvement. Shouldn't you be a member of this group of individuals?

The Law of Continual Success is one which respects the person who has an inner drive for never-ending breakthroughs, not for those who have placed limits over their own minds. Oh, what we would achieve if we allowed ourselves the liberty of exceeding our own selves! Sometimes, it is really easy to just place a cap over our own minds and stop succeeding, simply because we think that what we have achieved is good enough.

What can you attempt tomorrow that would make your success of today pale in comparison?

The cure for incessant pride about having arrived or achieved is to create new expectations for yourself which are currently beyond your own reach. If you do this, more resources—mental, physical, financial, and every other form of resource you need—would be pulled in your direction. However, if you decide to revel in your newfound position of greatness, don't be surprised if it starts to shrink and you are, once again, at the bottom of the ladder.

Keeping in mind that what is considered the ultimate success of today, the most ground-breaking thought, and most unique invention of today will be regarded as mediocre achievements tomorrow, should help remind you that no one invention cannot be exceeded or superseded. In fact, the invention of something gives license to the creation of something newer.

Don't Be Scared of Taking the Next Step.

Fear only attracts failure. Nothing else is capable of being drawn to fear. If you find yourself fearful, use the Law of Confession to redirect your thoughts back to those of a stable mind and of being bold and excellent!

Fear is terrible because it makes even those who have been able to achieve something great to flop and become redundant. Why? Because they are then scared of taking the next step! What they do not know is that taking the next step makes the Law of Attraction answer to you and allows continual success to be your standard!

Chapter 10

EMBRACING FORGIVENESS

"Would you let go of that hurt for your own sake?"

Total B...

The way that word tastes on my lips is as though it is easy to do, but anyone who has had to be on the giving end of this act knows that it is challenging. In essence, forgiveness is never an easy state to achieve. As much as it is peddled as being the greatest state of health and maturity, not one person can say that forgiveness is easy. In fact, it is complicated.

However, the Law of Attraction makes use of our vibes (as we have discussed in an earlier chapter). Now, the positive vibes of joy, peace, laughter, strength, goodness, greatness, and excellence—vibes which make us smile just by thinking about them—can only be achieved and maintained when we are free of bitterness.

Bitterness—both medically and non-medically speaking—seems to have the strength of its own creation, which makes it eat up anything in its way. Many lives have been consumed by bitterness. This is achieved by this terrible state coming up, sucking out all of the positive vibes, and replacing it rapidly with negative vibes of hopelessness, doubt, fear, and even depression. The cure is forgiveness.

Forgiveness is that vial through which positive energy can be created, emitted, and maintained. It makes it easy to live with almost anyone and to achieve great degrees of success. Before you begin to jump up and down with excitement at having discovered the key to living in excellence, you should be well aware of the fact that forgiveness is one of the most difficult states to achieve.

We have all experienced negative events and situations in our lives. Many of us are holding grudges and resentment toward individuals for these events that happened. Just by living, you have acquiesced to the fact that you would go through challenging and hurtful situations; that people would hurt you with their words and, moreso, people would intentionally place stumbling blocks in your way...inadvertently. This is the truth: It really is easy to hold onto a grudge. Very easy. By holding onto grudges, you are emitting self-defeating negative energy. Think about it. Let me remind you of what you're doing when you hold onto a grudge: You are simply canning up a lot of negative energy. You are bottling it up and, after a while, it will grow and become greater than the can in which you have placed it in. What, then, do you expect? That's right: It's going to grow and begin to eat you up!

For a moment, if you hold a grudge against someone, pause and allow yourself to think about this person. I can bet $1,000 on the fact that when you thought of this person, you didn't have any positive thoughts running through your brain at lightning speed. If anything, what you had were a conglomerate of negative thoughts as they swirled around in your head. Am I right?

I understand how hurt you feel about what was perpetrated against you, but I would like to let you know the equivalent of what you're doing: You are allowing a lot of negative energy to flourish in your being, the more you grant yourself access to think about them and hold that grudge against that person (or group of persons). I'm sure you must have heard that when you forgive someone, you are doing yourself a favor. You probably thought that was bullshit. Hold on: It is **NOT** bullshit. It is a universal law that when you free someone from the clutches of unforgiveness in your mind, those clutches become empty. Surely, you see that this reflects a state of utter freedom, right?

I agree with the veritable author, Ann Lamont, when she says: *"In fact, not forgiving is like drinking rat poison and then waiting for the rat to die."*

It feels unkind and unjust that the person who is hurt, as well as the one doing the forgiving, is one and the same. I know and am well aware that it hurts to have to let go of something that was probably really traumatizing for you. Even if you have held onto the grudge for years and think it is implausible for you to have to let go, I would like you to think of it this way: What if, by not forgiving the hurt perpetrated against you, you have prevented yourself from soaring? Holding someone in mental shackles creates a greater burden for you regarding takeoff and flying in life!

Think of the act of forgiving someone in this way: Throwing away all that accumulated garbage of negative emotions into a vast sea, forever letting go of that hurt. The refreshing sense of freedom that accompanies the state of forgiveness is probably unparalleled. You cannot have forgiven the hurts perpetrated against you and still feel bound. You might not even recognize the state of your mind anymore (especially if you have dwelt in unforgiveness for a really long time), but this is what you'll feel: inexplicable freedom. The longer you defer forgiveness, the longer you defer your own freedom—and the more you attract that negative state of mind and negative energies.

We would still get into gratitude later on, but we need to be grateful for even the bad things that have happened to use—for the terrible things we have been made to experience and for all of the hurt that has come to us from the hands of others. If we are careful and patient enough, we would even realize that with the pains of yesterday, we can build a castle today! With the disappointment and anger of today, we can build a mansion tomorrow! However, forgiveness is the key to the realization of all of this.

Pick Up Lessons from What Hurt You

In the process of recovery from hurt, you can also use this avenue to ruminate on the circumstances surrounding this occurrence and pick up vital life lessons from it. The reason for which this piece of advice might have been stoned had it been given while you were in a state of unforgiveness, is that this state blinds you from seeing anything good that could probably be a resultant effect of the pain which you had to bear.

This is one principle that must always guide your choices and decisions in life. There is always something to be learned from any situation, and you can grow—regardless of what befalls you. Those who have risen to become great individuals used the same things that were meant to have destroyed them: the hurt and harm perpetrated by others to build great stepping stones for their own success. This mere act has the capability of drawing to itself such high energy and positive vibration that you might not have thought existed in times past.

Forgive Yourself

While forgiving others is very important to growth and progress in life, there is something even more important: forgiving one's self.

We sometimes think that holding a grudge against ourselves for whatever wrong we feel we have perpetrated or against the mistakes of our past is just the 'thing to do.' Somehow, we think it is okay and, in fact, good, as it reminds us not to make such mistakes in the future. This is a huge lie. As a matter of fact, when you choose not to forgive yourself, what you have done is self-sabotaged your own forgiveness. This is because when you decide not to forgive yourself, you are your own enemy. You are both generating and absorbing significant amounts of negative energy and vibes.

To have the Law of Attraction work in a positive way for us, we need to forgive ourselves and let go of this self-sabotaging concept of holding ourselves in bondage to unforgiveness.

Carlene Randolph

Conclusion

Total B...

The 'Phenomenal Woman' is someone who understands that her scars are a mark of the warrior that she is. She realizes that often, she gets wounded so that she can then become stronger. When she fails, it is so that when she stands up, she is a better fighter—and winner. She is often broken before she is remolded.

Ever heard the story of the butterfly? The butterfly was once an egg, then larva, and then it grew into the pupa stage—all before it began to sprout wings and eventually become the butterfly we know. Some brilliant persons looked at the exciting changes in the life cycle of the butterfly and referred to it as 'Metamorphosis.'

As humans, we rarely view our lives as going in cycles, but indeed, we have those life cycles real in our beings. It is the reason we often feel stuck at certain points in our lives, as if nothing is going on or as if nothing is moving as it ought to. At other times, however, we are seemingly progressing at the speed of life. Many of these times, we forget or leave in the background those periods of peril—those times when our worlds were crashing down at our feet.

Don't forget. Remember those times when things seemed impossibly wrong. It helps you to linger in reflections, as you mentally persuade yourself that, indeed, all will be well.

This book was written to help you in the process of becoming whole and to make you see how life could be full and rosy—regardless of the circumstances that befall you and irrespective of the pressures of daily living you encounter daily.

For the average woman who has been alive for up to three decades or more, life will sometimes have brought you to your feet. You will have encountered sauntering moments that you felt you wouldn't survive.

How about you stop for just a moment to take in a deep breath?

How about you look into the future with purpose and clarity, reminding yourself that even if you feel pain now, that pain is only temporary?

How about you stop allowing your emotions to get numbed by circumstances to the point that you are only half of the woman you ought to be because you block out pain so much?

I am interested in you becoming whole because I am a woman who has stood where you once stood and have gone through some rather crippling experiences. Yet, I made it to the other side alive and strong. If I could do it, you can, too.

We are so capable of achieving greatness, which is perhaps one of the reasons we doubt ourselves so much because statistically, those who doubt themselves the most are the ones who are extremely capable of producing the best of the best results. Who you are is never on full display. Even if you have shown strength in the past, there's so much more within you that has not seen expression by the world.

The passion burning within you that makes you so able to express emotion is the same feature that will push you towards inexorable greatness.

Just like Marianne Williamson said, *"Our deepest fear is not that we are inadequate. Our deepest fear is that we are powerful beyond measure. It is our light, not our darkness that most frighten us. We ask ourselves, 'Who am I to be brilliant, gorgeous, talented, and fabulous?' Actually, who are you not to be? You are a child of God. Your playing small does not serve the world. There is nothing enlightened about shrinking so that other people won't feel insecure around you. We are all meant to shine, as children do. We were born to make manifest the glory of God that is within us. It's not just in some of us, it's in everyone. And as we let our lights shine, we unconsciously permit others to do the same. As we are liberated from our own fear, our presence automatically liberates others."*

There's so much truth packed in that quote that if we begin to dissect it, it would be impossible to get to the bottom of it. Still, if you go over it in your mind often enough, it would resonate deeply within you.

Stretch your mind! It would amaze you the immense capabilities packed into your single being. The world might try to limit you…your environment might try to limit you…but it would be a sad eventuality if you listen to those limiting thoughts, concepts, ideas, and ways of doing things.

Carlene Randolph

Ultimately, the greatest agony of life is the agony of not telling the story that's yearning for expression on the inside of you.

Stand up tall in the realization of who you are, and tower over those circumstances that have made you bow in regret!

www.ingramcontent.com/pod-product-compliance
Lightning Source LLC
Chambersburg PA
CBHW070521100426
42743CB00010B/1899